Prayers
Mantrams
— and —
Invocations

Selections from Torkom Saraydarian
and other sources

TSG Publishing Foundation, Inc.

Prayers, Mantrams and Invocations
(Includes *Five Great Mantrams of the New Age* by Torkom Saraydarian, first published in 1975)

© 2001 The Creative Trust

First printing by Aquarian Educational Group, 1975
Second printing by TSG Publishing Foundation, Inc., 2001
Third printing by TSG Publishing Foundation, Inc., 2007

All Rights Reserved: No part of this publication may be reproduced, stored in a retrieval system, or transmitted in any form, by any means, electronic, mechanical, photocopying, recording or otherwise, without permission in writing from the copyright owner or his representatives. Contact publisher for details.

ISBN10: 0-929874-87-0
ISBN13: 978-0-929874-87-6
Library of Congress Catalog #: 73-39431

Printed in the United States of America

Cover Design:	*Nurhan Thompson* Phoenix, Arizona
Printed by:	*Print Partner* Tempe, Arizona
Published by:	T.S.G. Publishing Foundation, Inc. Post Office Box 7068 Cave Creek, Arizona 85327-7068 United States of America www.tsgfoundation.org

Note: All spiritual and health information is given as a guideline. This information should be used with discretion and after receiving professional advice.

Foreword

This booklet represents the combining of two earlier releases: *Five Great Mantrams of the New Age* by Torkom Saraydarian and *Prayers, Mantrams, and Invocations* which is a collection from Torkom Saraydarian, Agni Yoga, and many other sources. We have released these wonderful selections in an easy to use bound format. We felt that the two together make a wonderful handbook for prayers and mantrams.

We hope you enjoy these selections. When a particular selection uses the word "man" it is not meant as gender specific, but as a generic term to denote mankind. Every effort has been made to credit the sources for their prayers and mantrams. We are deeply grateful for all authors and publishers.

TSG Publishing Foundation, Inc. publishes and distributes all of the creative works of Torkom Saraydarian. *The Torkom Saraydarian University* offers spiritual training courses on-site and by correspondence. For complete information regarding our products and services, please call or write to us, or see our website: www.tsgfoundation.org

Table of Contents

Part I - Five Great Mantrams 7-60

Part II - Prayers, Mantrams and Invocations
    (alphabetical order)

Accept my Arms 72
Affirmation 107
Affirmation of a Disciple 42
Almighty Power 91
Asatoma 97
As the One Sun 85
Beauty 77
Beauty in Your Life 78
Beauty of Infinity 79
Beloved Lord 97
The Blessing of the Beloved Kwan Yin 90
The Creator 65
The Crossroads 73
A Daily Discipline of Worship — in five parts 109
Dedication 84
Dedication of the Soul 91
Divine Love 80
Filled with Joy 99
Fusion 104
The Gayatri 48
Go in Beauty 78
The Great Hymn 76
The Great Invocation 13
Group Brothers 84
Group Worship 99

Help	79
I Love Thee, O Lord	76
Invocation for the United Nations	89
Invocation to the Solar Angel	87
Invoke Me	70
Invoking Angels	105
Joy, Bliss, and Peace	91
Joy Song	100
Lead us O Lord	110
Let Thy Prayer Be	75
The Light	102
Lighted Way	104
Living Flame	95
Living Sacrifice	81
Lord of Beauty	80
The Lord's Prayer	61
Lotus Flower	66
Love Each Other	94
Love of the Lord	88
Love to all Beings	95
Mantram of Peace	88
Mantram of the New Group of World Servers	85
The Messenger	63
Money for the Forces of Light	87
More Radiant	82
Mother	79
Mother of the World	75
My First Message	62
My Mantram	68
My Presence	65
O Great Spirit	83
Path to Infinity	100
Prayer for Purification	92
Prayer of Inspiration	93

Prayer of Protection	92
Prayer of Saint Francis of Assisi	86
Prayer on the way to the Sacred and Hallowed Dwelling	61
The Prayer to Shamballa	56
Preparedness	64
Pure Thought	70
The Resplendent Temple	62
Responsibility	101
River of Miracles	82
Salutations	94
Searching for You	97
The Self	77
The Server	103
Seven Gates	71
Seven Words	67
Solar Angel	104
The Sons of Men Are One (Mantram of Unification)	32
The Stars	98
Strength to my Heart	64
The Sun	86
Teacher	64
Thank You Lord	106
Thy Benevolence	66
Thy Country	70
To the Light	69
Unity	103
Veiled Her Face	72
Wings of Alaya	71
Wither my Hand	69
The Word	103
Your Beauty	80
Your Presence	96
Assorted short prayers	111

Part I
Five Great Mantrams

Throughout the centuries, many forms of prayers, mantrams, rituals, and invocations have been given to humanity. They have inflamed the emotions and thoughts of men and have led us toward the horizons of true survival, toward higher visions of divine achievement. They have formed, in a sense, a blueprint to be constructed, a goal to be attained, a task to be fulfilled.

These prayers or invocations first of all attract the aspirations, the visions, and the hopes of the best minds of the race. Then they slowly penetrate into the minds and hearts of the masses, creating in them new responses, new awakenings, and new determinations; and slowly, man advances higher and higher upon the path of unfoldment.

As an example, let us take an invocation given to our race long before our era:

O Thou, Who givest sustenance to the universe,
From Whom all things proceed,
To Whom all things return,
Unveil to us the face of the true spiritual Sun,
Hidden in a disc of golden light,
That we may know the truth,
And do our whole duty,
As we journey to Thy Sacred Feet.

We can imagine how great was the effect of this invocation on the people who used it in their meditations and in their vocal aspirations. We can expect that those who used it sincerely created in themselves a newer way of thinking, feeling, and acting and directed their eyes to That to Which everything returns.

The culture of mankind is the materialized form of all those great aspirations, which have been expressed in the human heart and soul throughout the centuries, and which produced the new civilizations and the new eras. In olden days these aspirations and urges were given to humanity by wise men who knew how to direct human emotions and thoughts through rhythmic prayers, invocations, solemn pledges, and even through parables or proverbs.

These prayers and invocations have two degrees of influence. In the first degree, the invocation or the prayer has a suggestive influence. It may be a group self-suggestion, and the person who uses it could release in himself a new urge toward a better life which surpasses his former self or state of being. In the second degree, it is a pure invocation which is directed toward a great Power about Whom there is no doubt in the user's mind.

Considering the first case, when an invocation or a prayer is repeated day by day, year after year, with attention and meditation, it produces a real change in man toward betterment. If we recite a prayer or an invocation, and meditate upon it, it creates a rhythm in our mental and emotional world. This rhythmic influence gradually becomes stronger and changes our way of living and acting. This is the reason why we repeat our national songs or anthems or vows, our different pledges and mottos so often. They really affect us and create in us a uniform orientation toward the goal of the invocation.

How much greater is the influence of a pledge or an invocation if it has behind it enthusiasm and the recognition of the goal to be achieved. When we truly have faith in the goal expressed through the invocation, when we are able to see the beauty that could be ours in working toward that goal, the rest will be easy because this will create in us sooner or later the strong determination to achieve that goal throughout our life.

In the second case, we not only have faith in the goal enunciated through the invocation, but also faith in That Which exists as the Source of Creation. When we are sounding an invocation, we are directing our whole being toward that great Existence and evoking a response from Him. We are directing our radar toward space, and we are getting our rays back, enriched with a new response. We are coming in contact with a higher level of consciousness, with a new source of inspiration and energy.

Throughout the ages the dimensions of prayer have shifted gradually onto higher levels. In the early ages the masses prayed for their physical and emotional needs. Then it became an aspiration for individual enlightenment and love, toward being led in right directions. Prayer then emerged from its personal limitations and became a prayer for the family, group, nation, and eventually a prayer for all humanity.

Thus, in the degree that the aim of prayer changed, so the wording of the prayer also changed, and in relation to these changes, the level and the target of the prayer was changed.

In past centuries we were asking, we were demanding, but in this space age, we are channeling the higher energies into the field of human endeavor. We know that space is an ocean of energy waves in which numerous currents meet, strengthen each other, and transmute or control one another.

Mystics in olden days used to say that the spark-light produced by the glow-worm would have its existence for centuries and centuries, and would float in space and expand; and that not only that light, but also every voice that is projected would continue its existence in some way.

We know that nothing in the universe is lost but only transformed, transmuted into different forms and expressed again in different ways. If not an atom is lost, it means that not a single energy wave is lost; and if not a single energy wave is lost, it means that none of our emotional and mental waves are lost; and if they are not lost, they continue their good or bad effect upon human conduct and life.

When we depart from our beloved ones, we use nice expressions, such as "Good journey" or "We wish your success" or "May God be with you." With these words we impart to them a protective aura or an inspiring wave, a source of sincere joy.

It is for the same reason that so many fathers and mothers pray that their children may be spared from dangers and temptations and live in the light of their highest dreams and visions. We know so many people who pray every morning and night for their beloved ones and for humanity as a whole, thus throwing into space a purifying energy wave, a blessing.

The effect of prayer, however, does not stop here. It is not only an expanding incense, an illuminating agent; it is also a beam of energy directed toward the Central Power, becoming a channel to that Power. Here we have an appeal and an answer: Invocation and Evocation.

When the need is clearly known, when the fiery aspiration to meet that need is aflame in the heart of the invoking one, then the answer is certain and timely. But who is That to Whom we appeal? He is the One in "whom we live and move and have our being." He is the Great Presence, the all penetrating Presence.

We live under the illusion that only man is conscious — man who is but an atom in the planetary existence. How much smaller will he appear if we compare him with a solar system or with the whole Cosmos. And if such an insignificant atom has its own consciousness, would it be right to think that a planet does not have its own consciousness, or a solar system does not have a consciousness of its own which controls its physical body, a body which comes into existence, lives, grows, and one day passes away as the human body does? This consciousness guides the activity of that huge Body, supports it and uses it in the great Cosmic Plan, as a human soul does its body.

Every cell in our body has its own individual life and consciousness and, collectively, a body-life and body-consciousness. Is this not the picture of that relationship which exists between the planet, the solar system, and man, who is an atom or cell in comparison to the planet or solar system? If this is true, then we can say that there is a Presence Who is everywhere and in everything and in which everything lives, breathes, and moves.

In some of our churches, above the altar, intuitive artists have painted a picture of a big eye. This is a wonderful symbol, showing the omnipresence of That Great Existence, but Who is He? The best minds of the race tell us that He is the Life. He is the great Consciousness which supports and nourishes everything.

They say also that everything is life. Everything is materialized, crystallized life, and Life is everywhere, from the atom to the limitless space. Space itself is Life, an ocean of life — electricity. And this great Life involves everything.

Throughout the ages wise people have told us that this Great Life has three aspects. These three aspects are present in every atom and cell. Although sometimes imprisoned, they are ever ready to be released. There is no lifeless matter or lifeless object. Everything is part of the Great Life and IS Life. Everything emerges from the one Life and returns to the same Life.

We are told that the whole creation is like a figure 8. The Creation starts from a formless "circle" and gradually goes up toward the formless circle. The Bhagavad Gita expresses this very beautifully in Ch. 2:28 when it says:

The Beings have no appearance at the beginning; at the midway stage they get appearance; at the end they disappear again.

So, through this great figure 8, life flows as an electrical current, materializing and dematerializing continuously, but remaining as a whole.

We are told again that He is the Light, the Love, and the Will. In other words, He is the creative power, the consciousness of unity, and the essence of the One Law from Whom radiate all cosmic, universal, planetary, and social laws in all their pure differentiations.

He is the creativity. He is the awareness, and He is the Law in every form and in every phenomenon.

Christians say that He is the Father, the Son, and the Holy Spirit — the one God.

There are people who also call Him the positive cosmic electricity, the negative electricity, and the light which emerges when they contact each other.

— 1 —
The Great Invocation

Stanza One
Given in 1935

> *Let the Forces of Light bring illumination to mankind.*
> *Let the Spirit of Peace be spread abroad.*
> *May men of goodwill everywhere meet in a spirit of cooperation.*
> *May forgiveness on the part of all men be the keynote at this time.*
> *Let power attend the efforts of the Great Ones.*
> *So let it be, and help us to do our part.*

Stanza Two
Given in 1940

> *Let the Lords of Liberation issue forth.*
> *Let Them bring succor to the sons of men.*
> *Let the Rider from the secret Place come forth,*
> *And coming, save.*
> *Come forth, O Mighty One.*
>
> *Let the souls of men awaken to the Light,*
> *And may they stand with massed intent.*
> *Let the fiat of the Lord go forth:*
> *The end of woe has come!*
> *Come forth, O Mighty One.*

The hour of service of the Saving Force has now arrived.
Let it be spread abroad, O Mighty One.

Let Light and Love and Power and Death
Fulfill the purpose of the Coming One.
The Will to save is here.
The Love to carry forth the work is widely spread abroad.
The Active Aid of all who know the truth is also here.
Come forth, O Mighty One, and blend these three.
Construct a great defending wall.
The rule of evil now must end.

Stanza Three
Given in 1945

From the point of Light within the Mind of God
Let light stream forth into the minds of men.
Let Light descend on Earth.

From the point of Love within the Heart of God
Let love stream forth into the hearts of men.
May Christ return to Earth.

From the centre where the Will of God is known
Let purpose guide the little wills of men —
The Purpose which the Masters know and serve.

From the centre which we call the race of men
Let the Plan of Love and Light work out
And may it seal the door where evil dwells.

Let Light and Love and Power restore the Plan on Earth.

This invocation is essentially a prayer, synthesizing the highest desire, aspiration, and spiritual demand of the very soul of humanity.

"No one can use this Invocation or prayer for illumination and for love without causing powerful changes in his own attitudes; his life intention, character and goals will be changed and his life will be altered and made spiritually useful."

Alice A. Bailey, *Discipleship in the New Age*, Vol. II, p.168.

The initial parts of the Great Invocation were given in 1935 and in 1940. In 1945 at the time of the June full moon in New York, the version that is presently in use was given. It is a prayer or an invocation which has now become a world invocation or a world prayer. It is broadcast every day over many radio stations and is in use in many churches and brotherhoods in many countries. It has been translated into many languages. Hundreds of people have written about this wonderful invocation. It is even available for use by the deaf and the blind.

People have expressed a sincere acceptance of this invocation because it contains an urgent message to all humanity, because the human heart is sensitive to sublime beauties, and because the world is in need of true leadership.

We are told also that these Three-in-One Energies, the Light, Love and Power, have their own individual foci, stations, or centers through which they express themselves and act, fulfilling the will of the Central Life. These three have their own centers in extra-planetary, inter-planetary, human, and atomic fields through which these three energies flow, keeping the whole creation alive in a sole Will.

The great prayer invokes these three energies through all the Kingdoms of Nature and toward extra-systemic fields where they are centralized with their own presence. It is the first time in the history of humanity:

a. That these three centers are invoked simultaneously by humanity,

b. That the energies required to meet the planetary needs are so clearly identified, and

c. That all methods are used to make this Invocation the only aspiration of humanity, everywhere, in every race, 'focusing the inchoate mass demand of humanity on the highest possible level.'

How to Recite this Invocation.

We know that when we repeat a prayer or an invocation, after a while we become mechanical. We utter the words and the sentences without conscious participation, and we reap no result.

At the time we say the Invocation we must proceed through the following steps:

1. A second of mental silence
2. Penetrative concentration on the meanings of the words
3. Creative visualization

Mental silence means detachment from former or new thoughts. Concentration means that we are trying to focus on each word without letting our mind waver, penetrating into the deeper layers of word meaning. Creative visualization is a process of handling energy and building communication with higher levels of being.

All the words we utter are charged with energy from the various levels of our being.

If our utterance is mechanical, the words have little power. If we are emotional, they have more power. When we penetrate into the true meaning of our words, they are charged with still more energy. If our consciousness or being is focused in higher planes while uttering the words, they carry stupendous energy with them and they spread creative effects in space for a long, long time.

When the Invocation is intoned by an enlightened group, we have the greatest tool in our hands to control and to handle the divine energies in the great Nature. Let us discuss the Great Invocation one paragraph at a time:

> *From the point of Light within the Mind of God*
> *Let light stream forth into the minds of men.*
> *Let Light descend on Earth.*

We can feel its strength and the need for this appeal when we observe with clear vision the condition of the world and see, in spite of increasing light, the darkness in which we live and move and breathe.

With these three lines we invoke the Light within the Mind of God — the Mind which is in every atom, in every living creature, in every man, in the whole universe, and in the greater Cosmos — so that the light of reality, the light of meaning, the light of value and righteousness, the light of understanding, may descend into the darkness of human relation and release the beautiful light in every form and reveal the greater Light until the day be with us.

It is this light which will dispel the darkness from our minds, words, behavior, and activities. For the first time the minds of men will be liberated through new understanding, in a new day's dawn. Men will look upon each other as brothers and Sons of Light fused in the mind of God, from which come all gifts and paths toward the beauty of greater achievements.

It is this light which, on a planetary scale, will burn and dispel our lies, hatreds, and hypocrisies, all of which are based upon our common selfish urges and interests. It is this light which will show us the meaning of life, the high calling, the Plan, the destination toward which we are traveling. It will enable us to live a life of light on the Path of Light.

One of the Sufi mystics once said:

*If you open the heart of any stone,
you will find a radiating sun.*

It is this Sun which is invoked — through all atoms, human beings, and universes. How great a vision will open in our souls if we use our creative imagination and see the coming civilization created with such light that the human mind is aligned with the Great Mind and becomes the creative agent for the Great Mind!

In esoteric literature we are told that Lord Buddha is the point of Light. He is living on the highest level of the Cosmic Physical Plane, and the Divine Mind is radiating its light through this great Lord of Wisdom throughout the world.

*From the point of Love within the Heart of God
Let love stream forth into the hearts of men.
May Christ return to Earth.*

With this verse we invoke the second Great Energy, the Energy of Love, the fountain of which is symbolically called the Heart of God. The Heart of God embraces the whole.

In every manifested form we have a point of love; we have a heart.

To give the simplest definition of love we may say that it is the fire of life in man which awakens the consciousness of unity and inspires him to sacrifice everything to achieve that consciousness of unity on larger scales and on higher levels of goodness and beauty.

In the progressive development of the human being, first he exists for himself, then gradually he recognizes the existence of objects, next he becomes aware of the family, the group, the nation, and later of humanity as a whole.

Gradually, with an enlightened consciousness, he penetrates into the depth of existence and intuitively affirms that he is only a cell in the body of the Great Existence — a cell which, in fact, is in communion with every part of that Great Existence. When he realizes all of this, he tries to identify himself with and know himself as that Great Life.

The invocation is directed first to the heart of every man, from which will pour out the love, the consciousness of unity — Love-Light. Such a man will become a great healer and a great liberator of human beings.

The Center of Love found in the Heart of God is first of all the heart of man, because the heart of man is the only door through which one can reach to the heart of humanity and have access to the Heart of God. Also the heart of man is the only fountainhead from which the love of God can pour consciously the liberating, transfiguring energy. And the heart of man is a path that leads to that Great Heart which is composed of the martyrs, saints, knowers, seers, the resurrected ones of every nation.

It is the Love embodied in that Center which is invoked in this second verse, so the Christ again may descend on earth to work out the blueprint which He laid down 2000 years ago. This time He will establish the universal Kingdom of God on earth.

To be able to do this, the inherent Christ in every human heart should "descend on earth" so that on earth there starts a new life, a life based on the consciousness of unity. This immanent Christ is not necessarily a religious man or a devotee. He can be a man, a living beauty, in any social field, a strong leader radiating with love; a man who is completely oriented to the happiness, success, and liberation of mankind; a man who is continuously in contact with the Great Life Whom we call God or Cosmic-Consciousness — beyond the limitations of time and space.

The immanent Christ is the path through which will reappear the universal Christ. As the sole leader and teacher, He will open a new way for humanity, leading to higher achievements and realizations of inner heights, inner Himalayas.

Unless we open the path within to the steps of the Inner Christ, the Hope of Glory, we cannot feel the presence of that Great Existence Who has been leading humanity onward for 2000 years as the vision of perfection, the living beauty. According to His promise He will appear again in the world.

May Christ return to Earth.

Who is Christ? He is "the leader of the Kingdom of God, Leader of the Victorious Church. He is the embodiment of the divine principle of Love, the first one to reveal to men the true nature of God," and He has never left us. As He said in Matthew 28:20, "lo, I am with you all the days, even unto the end of the age."

May Christ return to Earth.

Is it not imperative to intensify the invocation for Love on a greater scale? Is there any other way to solve our problems — problems in our homes, in our nations, in humanity?

All humanitarian aspirations, all plans for the betterment of human life in any field are the answers to this ongoing invocation for love and loving understanding. This will continue until Love dominates all our thoughts, feelings, and actions and demobilizes the forces of darkness, the forces of evil in the world. These are the forces that enslave the human heart, conscience, and expressions — by force, fear, money, glamors, and illusions.

The Heart of God, the Love of God, nourishes the human conscience and consciousness as a Sun. When the obstacles found between Him and humanity are eliminated, when our hearts become clean and more sensitive to higher impressions, we will have an unbroken relationship between Him and our hearts.

Christ is the Love Stream out of God's Heart. At the present time there are thousands in the world who feel His presence, His rays of love, by which they become inspired, become transfigured, and sacrifice themselves for the welfare of humanity. Imagine a world which will come into existence as the result of such an invocation!

God is Love.

The Master Djwhal Khul, in one of his books dictated to A.A. Bailey, says:

"The basis of all Logoic action is love in activity, and the fundamental idea on which He bases action connected with the human Hierarchy is the power of love to drive onward — call it evolution, if you like, call it inherent urge, should you so prefer, but it is love causing motion and urging onward to completion."

A Treatise on White Magic, p.115.

From the centre where the Will of God is known
Let purpose guide the little wills of men —
The Purpose which the Masters know and serve.

Perhaps this is the most difficult verse to understand, though most of the religions of the world have prepared a way of approach. All religions symbolically tell us that God has His own Will and that around His throne there are Entities of Fire Who are the immediate interpreters of His Will. These great Existences formulate His Will and implement the Purpose.

This Purpose stands as a magnetic center which draws to itself all creation, each part according to its own capacity.

We are told that all the true laws given to the world are the precipitations of that mighty Center where the Will of God is known. These laws, as given in Holy Books, direct the human conduct — in individual and in group ways — toward the Central Magnet.

This is, in my mind, like a great symphonic orchestra, in which the conductor is teaching a symphony to each section of instruments (kingdoms of Nature), then trying to bring the whole together, gradually creating the ultimate rhythm and harmony that expresses the essential meaning of the symphony.

Each law, in any period, anywhere, is a way of translation of the central Will, on a given level, through a given culture or civilization. The governments, mostly through their legislation, are remote echoes of the Will of God, if they are not aberrated by their own separative intentions. All true leaders receive their inspiration and courage from that Center, mostly unconsciously, but in rare cases consciously. This is the Center which propels forward, and at the times of crisis the energy of the divine will becomes active within those who are dedicated to the welfare of humanity.

We are told also that in every human being there is a field of consciousness which is the vehicle of the divine will. If men could penetrate that level of consciousness, they could become impressed by the divine will. It is sometimes called the inner chamber into which a man must enter and, after closing the "doors and windows," speak to God in intimate privacy.

From the human point of view, "the centre where the Will of God is known" is the supreme focus of the highest aspirations and visions of all seers and martyrs, of the past and of the future. It is this center which must condition all the activities of men upon physical, emotional, and mental planes. Christ called this Center His "Father's house" — where the Father's Will reigns.

This great prayer invokes the Will of God so that "purpose guides the little wills of men."

We learned to say, "Let Thy Will Be done in heaven and on earth." We refer to the same Center, the same Fountain, the same Energy — trying to align and to harmonize our little wills with His Will. The secret of everlasting peace and understanding among all nations rests in identifying the human will with the divine will. All our miseries, wars, and sufferings are the result of the friction between our own will and God's Will.

Freedom is not a process of getting away from that Will. On the contrary, freedom is an act of approaching and identifying with that Will. The closer you approach it, the more you become free. The farther you depart from that Will, the more you enter into misery and enslavement.

If we observe the life of the planet, we see that humanity as a whole throughout the ages evolved on the planet, a little here, a little there; physically, then on the emotional level, then on the mental level; first individually, then in group formation, then as a whole on the universal scale.

With the advance of science, people observed how humanity and the universe are conditioned by immutable Laws. These Laws are present not only on the cosmic level but also in solar, planetary, human, cellular, and atomic fields. There is only one Law, and all the laws are subdivisions of that great Law.

All existence is evolving, going toward an unknown Purpose. A Central Magnet is drawing everything toward Himself. Is this not the reason why all the cleavages eventually lead us to unity, all the resistance to light ultimately creates more light, all dictatorship increases the urge to freedom, all hatred finally produces more love and understanding? So, the True, the Beautiful and the Good are imminent and are the aspects of that Central Will.

> *From the centre which we call the race of men*
> *Let the Plan of Love and Light work out*
> *And may it seal the door where evil dwells.*

Here the human race as a whole is taken as a center, a field of energy where the Plan of Love and Light must work out.

If we look at the human race as a whole, we see a picture of continuous upheaval in which contradictory forces, activities, and directions meet, creating an impassable chaos in all fields. This chaos can be turned into a cosmos only through love and light.

What is the Plan of Love, the Plan of Light?

The first can be formulated by the words, "Love your fellow man as yourself."

The second: "Search for the truth and the truth will make you free."

Much of humanity has reached a stage where individuals dream and plan a creative life of a new age. They dream of a good and beautiful life under the sun, free from hatred and ignorance.

This fourth verse may be called the summary of age long human aspirations, visions, and hopes. All these are directed to the Cosmic Consciousness as an invocation so that the powers of Love and Light can "seal the door where evil dwells."

The word "evil" refers to all forces which hinder the progress of humanity. The door of evil, from which emerge those forces which prevent the liberation and unity of humanity, is not open only in the hearts of individuals but also in nations and in humanity as a whole.

The evil recognized in the present is materialism, the spirit of separation, and totalitarianism. Totalitarianism is our worst enemy in all departments of human life. This is an evil the door to which must be sealed, or, in other words, its activity must be stopped.

These three forces are acting as three evil forces in governments, in churches, in groups, and in nations. Most of the miseries of the world are the result of these three forces. They foster injustice, fear, and hatred with their resultant tears and bloodshed.

Is it timely to say: "May it seal the door where evil dwells"? If we visualize the misery of the coming ages as a result of these three dark forces, then this invocation becomes the deepest call of the human heart.

Let Light and Love and Power restore the Plan on Earth.

The last verse synthesizes the invocation and, as a great symphony, ascends toward the Central Heart.

We are told that

"The whole order of nature evinces a progressive march toward a higher life. There is a design in the action of the seemingly blindest forces. The whole process of evolution with its endless adaptations is a proof of this."

H.P. Blavatsky, *The Secret Doctrine*, Vol. I, p. 298.

There is a plan behind all creation. We cannot imagine laws without a plan, a plan without a purpose, nor a purpose without an Originator — "the Centre where the Will of God is known." This is the department where higher intelligences study the will of God, the Purpose of God.

The center which we call the love center of God is the Kingdom of God, having as its leader that great Individual Whom we call the Christ. This is the department where the Purpose of God changes into the Plan for our planetary life. Humanity, the third center, will work out the Plan through its seven main departments: politics, education, communication and philosophy, the arts, science, religion, and finance.

Every man has a high calling. The most sacred duty of each man is to find that high calling within himself, unveil it, and release it in its full expression in his daily life.

The Ageless Wisdom suggests that the high calling of each man is a portion given to him from the Great Plan, one strand of the Great Fabric, and that Plan is the high calling of all humanity. Move closer to your soul, and the Plan will gradually be unveiled. Your soul is a part of the Great Plan.

It is not an easy task to establish the kingdom of love and light within a man or a group. Humanity as a whole, through agony and suffering, is emerging from the night of ages and is moving toward the light and day of the future.

This Invocation is the prayer for the Future—that great Future when humanity will bloom to its highest beauty and express the music of the Purpose of the Infinite.

As I enter into my private room and sit on my chair to begin my daily meditation, I close my eyes and visualize millions and millions of people who, with a single vision, are standing in a boundless field and sounding the Great Invocation with me.

I hear the voice of humanity as a great oceanic roar rising to the sky, and then, suddenly, the lightning flashes! The veil of cloud is pierced, unveiling the true Spiritual Sun.... I see a path extending from humanity to the Spiritual Sun and the Christ climbing upward through each human heart, lifting every man to His highest destiny.

Let Light and Love and Power restore the Plan on Earth.

The Great Invocation is a mantram, a word of power.

When you have climbed the first great peak of your being and have entered into communication with your Solar Angel, on that mountain top you will sound The Great Invocation with clear attention, with fiery aspiration, and with creative visualization.

Mantrams or invocations are more effective when they are sounded on the highest mental levels and this takes preparation, alignment, and Soul-infusion. This is the first music that the Soul-infused personality will play, or sound, and through it the lower vehicles will be charged with great energies of light, love, and power.

Actually, the act of sounding the invocation is an act of extending the alignment toward the centers of light, love, and power.

The Teaching states that there are three great Lords Who represent these three great centers of energy, and They form a Triangle at the center of which Christ stands. These Lords are

- The Avatar of Synthesis, a Cosmic Being Who represents the Center of Power
- The Spirit of Peace, Who represents the Center of Love
- The Lord Buddha, Who represents the Center of Light

When we sound this holy mantram, we invoke these three great Lords, from whom stream forth light, love, and power. Here we can use our visualization to deepen our alignment with these three great centers and evoke the needed energies to "restore the Plan on earth."

We are in one-pointed focus. The alignment has been achieved between the Soul and its vehicles. Now we use our visualization to see how light is descending and radiating in response to our invocation and clearing away the illusions and darkness found within men and within the universe. What a great change is occurring in our social, economic, and political fields as this light is descending and radiating!

With the next verse we are visualizing the Heart of God, the great Lord of Love. What great preparations He is undergoing to return to earth! See how the energy of Love is streaming forth into the hearts of men, creating fundamental changes within humanity as a whole, and establishing right human relations throughout the planet. See how love is melting all mountains of hatred, of exploitation, of war materials and war machines all over the world; the people of the world are becoming really human, and the New Age of Brotherhood is on its way.

Then you see how the Purpose of God is guiding the little wills of men and creating a new world in which men are consciously entering into the mysteries of Initiation and becoming co-workers of that Purpose.

At the fourth verse you will visualize humanity as one center in which the Plan of the Hierarchy is working and sealing the door where evil dwells — evils of hatred, separation, evils of totalitarianism, evils of materialism, evils of war, and evils of ignorance.

You may extend your vision and invoke the light, love, and power, but without creating specific, limited thoughtforms. Your visualization will be general, not particular, as we do not know really what kind of world we will have in detail. If we create details and particular thoughtforms according to our level of sensitivity and understanding, we may build obstacles to the manifestation of the Plan.

Sounding the Invocation

Sometimes it will be very effective if you imagine that someone, a higher being, a great initiate, is sounding the Great Invocation and you are repeating it after, verse by verse.

To make it more potent, you listen to the whole verse and repeat it in one breath, but without haste. Pause for three counts after the first verse, seven counts after the second verse, nine counts after the third verse, and twelve counts after the fourth verse. In these silent periods, mentally concentrate and visualize the effect of the preceding verse.

The effect of our invocation depends on the level from which we are speaking or sounding it.

If a man's consciousness is focused on the physical level only, the vocal effect of his invocation will be very weak and will not bring permanent results.

If his consciousness is focused on the emotional plane, his invocation or speech will carry more force and bring greater results.

If he is focused on the mental plane, then his invocation will be still stronger, will have more force and evoke higher responses.

If his focus is in the higher mental and Intuitional Planes, he is a white magician and his invocation and speech is charged with very high voltage energy. He is able to be highly creative in line with the Plan. That is why the alignment is so necessary. If the alignment is done properly and the consciousness is lifted up to the higher mental planes, then the pilgrim has more energy at his command and his invocation is able to reach the Great Centers and bring in light, love, and power for the enlightenment of humanity and for the fulfillment of the Plan.

It will greatly help us if in our leisure time we take this Invocation and reflect on each sentence, each verse, to increase our understanding of its esoteric meaning. Words spoken or sounded in understanding create greater effects and extend our focus of consciousness into the higher planes of our being.

"At this time, the *Great Invocation* is the greatest aid to humanity. The fulcrum, the axis of the *Great Invocation*, is Christ — the reappearance of the great Lord, Christ.

Great Teachers, such as H. P. Blavatsky, Master Djwhal Khul, and Master M., tell us that Christ is a living individual, a living human being Who, because of His unparalleled progress, became the Head of the Hierarchy. He will hold that position for another two thousand years.

We are told that He is presently living in a very isolated spot in the Himalayas, serving humanity on various planes of existence. Thousands of people have contacted Him as they passed through their first and second initiations.

Some people like the *Great Invocation* because of its vision and power, but they do not like to use the word "Christ." They give themselves permission to change the *Great Invocation*, which was not origianted by them. Changing or deleting the Name of Christ eliminates the focus of the energies. It can even be harmful to those who use the *Great Invocation* for their personal or group advantages.

Those who, with good intentions, want to change the *Great Invocation*, would do better to create a totally different invocation of their own — instead of distorting a masterpiece painting with their unskilled brush.

The Most important and powerful line of the *Great Invocation* is:

May Christ return to Earth.

Curiously enough, it is this line which is under attack. By changing this formula, the Great Invocation no longer exists. This is what the distorters want.

When you are voicing,

May Christ return to Earth,

put all your aspiration and heart into your voice, visualizing at the same time that you are expressing the aspirations of a great number of people."

Triangles of Fire, by Torkom Saraydarian, pp. 76-77

— 2 —

The Sons of Men Are One

This is a beautiful mantram, and it is called "The Mantram of Unification."

> *The sons of men are one and I am one with them.*
> *I seek to love, not hate;*
> *I seek to serve and not exact due service.*
> *I seek to heal, not hurt.*
>
> *Let pain bring due reward of light and love.*
> *Let the soul control the outer form*
> *And life and all events,*
> *And bring to light the love*
> *Which underlies the happenings of the time.*
>
> *Let vision come and insight;*
> *Let the future stand revealed.*
> *Let inner union demonstrate and outer cleavages*
>   *be gone.*

Let love prevail.
Let all men love.

The Externalisation of the Hierarchy by Alice A. Bailey, p. 142.
(The first line is *The souls of men are one....* in A. A. Bailey's Unfinished Autobiography, p. 290)

Is it possible to relay this message to everyone in the world and enable each one to understand the beauty of it?

We are told that ideas or visions change men and the world and create a new culture and a new civilization.

There are ideas and visions which impose themselves upon our consciousness and demand actualization. There are ideas and visions which meet the needs of humanity at a given period or cycle to further its progress on the path of perfection. No intelligent person can reject these ideas because on them depends his survival and his enjoyment of life.

The mantram quoted above presents such a powerful vision and ideas that if a man really tunes in with them all his persona, family, group, and social attitudes will change forever.

How will a man act, feel, think, serve, and labor if he really accepts the teaching that "*the sons of men are one, and I am one with them*"? Life on this planet will not survive unless we realize this. And if we come to accept it we will find greater joy and success in living.

Pause a moment and consider that you are really going to live according to the ideas presented in the above two lines. What changes would occur within you and within the field in which you live or work? All virtues and joys of life originate from ideas such as "the sons of men are one." Humanity is like a huge individual within whose body all men and women are cells with different levels and different functions but with a sense of unity which guarantees the success and survival of all.

I am one with them.

If I am one with them, am I living my life according to that vision or idea? Through what psychological, social, and even physiological changes must I pass in order to actualize that concept? Is discipline needed? Yes, and a heavy one. Are sacrifices needed? Yes, and increasingly so. Might I experience rejections, perhaps loss of my position or social reputation? Not at all. People everywhere, in all walks of life, are becoming aware that humanity is one, that we are already late in coming to recognize this. They understand that only through the acceptance of the concept of one humanity can our energy, territorial, racial, religious, and communication problems be solved. Whether we like it or not, humanity is progressing toward unity. World-wide communication systems and international cooperation in many fields are on the increase. The United Nations with its various branches, great formations of nations — such as the United States, Russia, the United Kingdom, China — and many scientific and commercial corporations have become realities on this planet. Is this not proof that the concept of the unity of mankind is becoming universally accepted?

Undoubtedly the proponents of this concept will face some opposition, but opposition can be overcome when one really demonstrates in his life his oneness with mankind.

The people of the new era will love you; everywhere they will be impressed by the idea of oneness. What is needed is courage and freedom from all thoughts that limit your radiation.

You must demonstrate with your own life.

I seek to love, not hate.

Can you imagine the beauty of a man who will make a pledge with himself not to hate, but to love? Not to hate anybody? This does not mean that he will not be able to see faults in some people, but this fact will not lead him into hatred but to greater love, understanding, and labor.

Never in the history of humanity have problems been solved by hatred. Hatred produced only failure, destruction of cultural masterpieces, massacres, slaughter, destruction of moral and spiritual values, economic depressions, crises, and increased physical and psychological diseases.

Everything beautiful in the world is the product of true love. All beautiful objects that have been preserved are the products of love, not of hatred.

I seek to serve and not exact due service.

"What an illogical idea!" exclaims the greedy individual. But this is the only concept that will prevent us from slipping into the abyss of exploitation. Those who exploit others will themselves eventually be exploited.

Service is not only a labor. It is a labor of love given with the awareness of unity. When you render a service, don't you feel offended if the beneficiary tries to repay you? The rendering of a service without expectation of reward releases an immense joy in your heart. This joy is a healing energy, an uplifting energy, an enlightening energy and a unifying energy. There are psychological diseases which cannot be cured unless the affected person learns how to overcome them by seeking to serve and not exacting due service.

Sometimes you have good neighbors who want to serve you. Perhaps you once had a blowout on a freeway and a stranger stopped and fixed your tire and continued on his way without expectation of even your thanks. He did it because he felt that you are he and he does not need recognition.

I seek to heal, not hurt.

This is the feeling of all people of the new era.

Once I went to a garden to pick a flower. As I stretched out my hand a little boy about five or six years of age shouted, "No! Your can't kill that flower!" I froze. What an affirmation of love and what a sense of unity was demonstrated by that little angel!

Does hurting help us? Why then enjoy hurting people? Why then hurt without considering the damage we do?

Think about war. Think about concentration camps. Think about genocide. Think about the cruelty which is prevalent everywhere. Think about vivisection. Think about prison conditions and the conditions of the prisoners. How did all these come into being? With them came expenses, increasing our taxes by millions of dollars. These evils came about because we did not live according to the vision.

I seek to heal, not hurt.

No complications in our social life can be solved by hurting; only by healing can we solve them — healing on all planes: physical, emotional, and mental. Hurting will only deepen the wounds of our life.

No man can hurt another without hurting himself, and no man can heal another without experiencing a great joy and bliss in his heart. Why deprive ourselves and others of such a blessing which can come only through love, service, and healing?

Let pain bring due reward of light and love.

What pain is this? The pain of the wounded on battlefields. The pain of those who lost their loved ones. The pain of those who lost their homes. The pain brought about by the destruction of cities and cultural monuments. Yet all these pains lead us to the understanding of the causes of pain and to cooperation with each other to alleviate and even prevent such causes.

Understanding the cause is light.

Cooperation to eliminate the cause is love.

What will be the reward? Increased understanding of the cause of pain and suffering.

Do we need to suffer to know the causes of our suffering? We do not need to suffer when we understand why we are suffering.

There are many pains in life which have not yet been controlled, but there do exist pains the causes of which can be eliminated. Is not one of the greatest desires of the human being to eliminate pain upon learning that the pain was the result of ignorance and hatred? If we learn to understand and cooperate, we will be rewarded by the knowledge that our pain and the pains of millions have not been endured in vain.

Let the soul control the outer form, and life, and all events.

The soul in us is the sense of unity. As we have a sense of smell, a sense of taste, a sense of touch, etc., so also do we have a sense which can be called the soul. This sense is the sense of unity. It operates for unity, and it is expressed only by acts of unity because it stands for unity.

A man's soul is the eye of his True Self, and this eye when opened sufficiently can see only unity in the diversity of forms. It sees the essence which expresses itself in manifold ways, means, colors, and forms.

Let this sense control our outer form, and life, and all events. Let all these be expressions of soul, of harmony, with the interests of all at heart. Let our mouths speak the language of the soul. Let our feet walk the path of the soul. Let our minds operate in the light of the soul, and let all events be expressions of that inner sense of beauty and unity.

And bring to light the love that underlies the happenings of the time.

Underlying the happenings of the time are the law of justice, the law of cause and effect, and love. Love is not a sentiment but rather a universal law which underlies the waves of the ocean of life. It is not the direct cause of waves (happenings) but it underlies all waves and motion. The waves and agitation are caused by various agents, but the ocean remains as one whole. Let our soul, one of our higher senses, bring us to the understanding that no matter how threatening the waves of the events are, eventually they will subside because the divine love is the ocean and that love eventually will enlighten us and enable us to understand the purpose for which we have been placed on this planet in this little solar system.

Let this love come into light. Let us see it, sense it, and live it, and thereby eliminate the miseries of the earth caused by lack of love. For example, all philanthropic movements, all achievements of cooperation among nations, all research, all urges to transcend our limitations of time and space, all efforts to heal the sick, educate the people, and to guide the youth, all movement toward spiritual unfoldment, all efforts to approach the Hierarchy, all endeavors to pave the way for the reappearance of Christ, and all activities to spread the Ageless Wisdom which is the root of all religions and philosophies all are this great love which underlies the events of our time.

Love is active; it has plan, purpose, and determination; and it is the energy that will lead us from Chaos to Beauty. Once we realize this fact, our energy and courage to stand for right human relations, for truth and righteousness, will increase a thousand-fold and we will stand as disciples of great causes for one humanity.

Let vision come and insight.

Vision is the future, the blueprint within us which is going to be manifested, come into expression, come to life. The seed will grow toward its culmination, to its high limit of beauty. It is this future for ourselves, this future for humanity, which must dawn in our eyes, and we must see that the future of a human being is a process of entering into ever-progressing light of glory. I define glory as the synthesis of all our virtues and spiritual powers.

How marvelous one will feel if suddenly he sees the vision of a fountain that he is planning to build! A vision of beauty, a vision of the future. Are we not going to have greater ecstasy if we can realize that this spoiled young girl or boy one day will metamorphose into one of the great heroines or heroes of service for humanity? Can we foresee how he or she will change, develop, overcome, strive, and eventually find his or her path toward Infinity? What a power you acquire when you have developed your insight sufficiently to see this vision!

Insight is the ability of the inner eye to see the future, the prototypes of things to come. Insight develops as the vision is formed on the inner planes.

Once a human being acquires the vision and insight, the future stands revealed.

A friend told me a story about a gold miner who came to California with a million dollars worth of equipment. He dug and dug, seeking to reach the ore, but eventually gave up after having reached the conclusion that he was mistaken in his choice of land. His neighbor bought all his equipment for much less than the original price. After the former owner had departed he started to dig. The ore was only three feet deeper. What a great richness the original owner would have had if he had vision and insight! It is vision and insight that gives us patience, endurance, and persistence.

Let inner union demonstrate and outer cleavages be gone.

Let the inner union, which is a reality, demonstrate itself in our minds and in our lives. Let us see the signs of this inner union.

Is my body a union? What about my personality, my physical, emotional, and mental nature? Can they survive if an inner union does not exist in them?

Can't we say that sanity, health, creativity, beauty, and joy are the demonstrations of our inner unity? Let this inner union demonstrate itself as cooperation in humanity, as health, creativity, beauty, joy, and love in humanity, and let "outer cleavages be gone."

There is no inner cleavage, only outer cleavages. Only on the surface, not in the depth of life can you find cleavages. All cleavages eventually will change into diversity of colors and sound and form the supreme symphony of Cosmos.

Let love prevail. Let all men love.

Is it possible to find a greater wish, a greater desire, a greater aspiration for humanity than this burning command?

Let love prevail. Let all men love.

How can we do this when we see daily the crimes in movies, on television, and on our streets everywhere? The answer is very simple. Love more. Let love prevail in your life. Let it increase year after year. Let it embrace all humanity, all living beings. Then you will be a fiery magnet drawing other beings into the line of love. Eventually all men will love because the essence of all men is love.

— 3 —
Affirmation of a Disciple

The act of affirmation is an awakening to one's True Self, into the reality of his essence. Man is not as he appears to be; he is beyond his vices and virtues, his joys and suffering.

Affirmation acts as a reminder to the conscious man of what his True Self is and, acting as a great, magnetic vision, it reestablishes his confidence in himself.

Man's consciousness often identifies itself with the phenomenal self and sometimes it sees the true nature of man and identifies itself with it. It is at this moment that our consciousness becomes creative. Creativity is the process of identification with reality and impressing the non-reality with the image of reality. Each time we experience a creative moment we establish a contact with reality, impressing our contact upon our brain and upon our senses.

Affirmation is also a process of detachment from things with which we formerly had been identified.

Affirmation may be compared to the building of a bridge which will enable the lower-oriented man to ascend to his True Self.

Affirmation is a process of releasing the energies of the inner Self and flooding the lower man with healing and harmonization.

Master Djwhal Khul gave us a magnificent affirmation used in olden days on the path of discipleship and initiation.

(See *Discipleship in the New Age*, Vol. II, p. 229, by Alice A. Bailey)

> *I am a point of light within a greater Light.*
> *I am a strand of loving energy within the stream*
> *of Love divine.*

*I am a point of sacrificial fire, focused within the
  fiery Will of God.
And thus I stand.*

*I am a way by which men may achieve.
I am a source of strength, enabling them to stand.
I am a beam of light, shining upon their way.
And thus I stand.*

*And standing thus revolve
And tread this way the ways of men,
And know the ways of God.
And thus I stand.*

Master Djwhal Khul says that "it has been used by disciples in the Masters' Ashrams for thousands of years, and is today given out by me to all true disciples."

After translating it into English He says, "This is the best I can do with words and phrases as I attempt to translate into language words so ancient that they antedate both Sanskrit and Senzar"!

I am a point of light within a greater Light.

I am not a man of darkness. I am not matter. I am not my body, my emotions, or my mind. I am not my pains and pleasures. I am not my money, my car, my property. I am a point of light.

When this is strongly affirmed you will feel the scattered light of your being coming into focus in your higher nature. You are creating a synthesis; you are becoming together. You are elevating yourself from a life that is based on form into a life that is rooted in light. You are affirming your true identity. You are discarding all the images of your false Self.

I am a point of light....

Like a star? Yes.
Like a flame? Yes.
This is you: a point of light free from all that causes you pleasure and pain.

Within a greater Light.

You are not in a great darkness but in a greater light because the light of the Almighty One is the ocean in which you are a point of light. You are a note in the Cosmic Symphony — a note that vibrates bliss, joy, and beauty.

I am a strand of loving energy....

I am not hatred. I am not a self-seeking person. I am not a revengeful man. I am not an ungrateful man. I am not a forgetful man. I am a loving energy. I spread joy, beauty, bliss, compassion. I bring together. I do not scatter, separate, divide but unify, synthesize, and heal.

Within the stream of Love divine.

I am not alone. My existence is in the stream of Love divine, I was created in love, I am traveling in love, I am going toward the ocean of love.

I only want to remind myself that I am Love and I know that all acts, feelings, and thoughts contrary to love will give way and gradually disappear. I will overcome them with the living stream of divine Love.

I am a spark of sacrificial fire,

focused within the fiery Will of God.

I exist as a fire in which all that is not fire will burn away. All illusion, expectation, and separative interests will turn into ashes. I will sacrifice them in the name of my True Self.

But I am not a flame by itself. I am a flame in the furnace of God's Will, the source of all energies, rays, powers, by which all creation, the whole manifestation is emanated, to which everything eventually returns.

That source is fire — fiery will. Nothing can hinder its way. I am a spark of sacrificial fire. I make everything sacred. Everything that I touch is made to live a purposeful life, to serve its purpose, in harmony with the whole. Being a fiery will in myself, my body conditions, my emotional and mental conditions must not affect my progress toward self-fulfillment. I, as the fiery will, will pave the way of self-determination, self-actualization, self-mastery burning and purifying all that hinders the spiritual realization.

As a fire my task is to cause transmutation, transformation, and transfiguration. I am a fire, not flesh, not bones, but the fiery life using this body to spread the fire by liberating energies of tiny sparks everywhere.

…and thus I stand.

I do not change or flicker. I am firmly established within the reality of my True Self, and I live and express myself as a spark of sacrificial Self, giving purifying fire everywhere I go and nothing can change me.

I am a way by which men may achieve.

All my communication and relations with people have one purpose: that I may help them to achieve — to achieve spiritual maturity, to achieve a state of pure awareness about the reality within their forms, to achieve self-mastery, to have greater creativity, beauty, joy, and bliss.

I am not an obstacle on the path of others nor of myself. I am not a wall. I am not a dead-end street, but a way for everything in everything. When people are lost in their dreams, I am a way to reality. When they fall into the prison of selfhood, I am a way out. When they lose their way, I am the way home. I am a way leading them toward the mountains, rivers, oceans, freedom, toward the festivals of brotherhood and unity.

I am a source of strength, enabling them to stand.

I do not kick the weak ones. I do not step on them to increase my selfish interests. I do not run away from my brothers. I stand with them, I encourage them, I show them their future, give them spiritual hope. I pass them my enthusiasm, my courage, my heart's energy, my love. I strengthen their vision, heal their wounds, equip them with necessary ideas, and put them on the road again. I do not make them lean upon me, to use my feet and hands, but to stand on their own feet and with courage and determination continue the path.

I am a source of strength.

Because I am my Self, I am not losing energy in ugly imagination, in day dreaming, in wrong thinking, in hate, in jealousy, in worry, in greed. I do not waste my energies in activities that do not further my mastery over my vehicles, do not help others to grow and to be creative. I know the value of my energy and I use it goal-fittingly.

Arrows of ill-thoughts cannot penetrate me as I have the shield of my compassionate heart.

I am a beam of light, shining upon their way.

If there is darkness on their path, I shed my light, myself — a beam of light, my knowledge, intuition, reality, courage, enthusiasm, ecstasy, beauty, and in my light, they see their light, and walk on their own path.

And thus I stand.

I keep being light, love, and power. I keep being my True Self.

And standing thus, revolve....

I do not only keep being light, love, and power, but I also put myself to the service of those who need me. I revolve. I shine with all my being, everywhere, in everything, north, south, east, west, above, below. I am like a sphere of light, love, and power and I revolve around the axis of God in me.

...and tread this way the ways of men.

I meet them on all their ways. I understand them. I see their motives and the causes of their actions, but always in my relationship with them I keep in my mind *"and know the ways of God,"* so that I do not follow the paths of men, but the ways of God within them.

And thus I stand.

I stand in full determination and bliss, so that "the evil is sealed, frustrated, and rendered futile."

— 4 —
The Gayatri

"Above the stratum of earthly thoughts stream the currents of the sun's wisdom, and in these regions begins the great pre-ordained Teaching. We summon to the encompassment of the Universe. But only the instrument of consciousness will permit the new experiments of the blending of spirit and matter."

Agni Yoga Society, *Leaves of Morya's Garden*, Vol. II, p.43.

The Gayatri is considered to be the most sacred verse of *Rig Veda* and is taken from the third of the ten cycles of hymns of *Rig Veda,* the cycle of the Rajaputra sage, Vishmamitra. (*Rig Veda* III 62.10)

The *Sanskrit* version of the Gayatri reads as follows:

OM.
Bhur Bhuva Svah
Tat Savitur Varenyam
Bhargo devasya dhimahi
Dhiyo yonah prachodayat.

A literal translation is:

OM
Earth, Mid-world, Heaven,
That life-sun's adorable
Light of God, let us meditate,
Souls, may enlighten us.

The free translation may read:

All of you, who are on earth,
Mid-world and Heaven,
Let us meditate
Upon the light adorable
Of the divine sun of life
Which may enlighten our souls.

The word *Gayatri* means to sing out or protect.

It is very interesting to realize that the Gayatri is a call to all beings found on objective and subjective planes to meditate every day at sunrise and sunset upon the Central Spiritual Sun of the Solar Life and the Monad in each human being. The only refuge for a man is his own innermost Self. Once a man achieves such a realization his life sings of beauty, grace, wisdom, love, peace, and bliss.

The Central Spiritual Sun is the source of the true Teaching, the light which penetrates into the three worlds of human endeavor, namely, the physical, emotional, and mental, and into the three planes of worlds of the universe, namely, physical world, astral world, and mental world.

As this Supreme Light descends into the darker regions of manifestation it fades out.

The invocation of the Gayatri tunes us in with this essence of light in the three worlds and, as the consciousness of man becomes open to the light through meditation, the light increases and the human consciousness expands and eventually enlightenment is achieved.

The three worlds to which the Gayatri refers are the lower vehicles of the Central Spiritual Sun within which live entities with corresponding bodies. The Gayatri invokes these entities to be ready for a group meditation upon the source of their beauty, the Sun of life, the Supreme light. In such a meditation it will be possible to reach the Source and draw the light down to the three worlds, establishing therein the paths of light as guides for all our activities on these three planes.

The principle ideas in the Gayatri are

    A. Synchronous meditation with other beings

    B. The existence of the Sun of Life

    C. Illumination or enlightenment of our souls

We can also divide the mantra into three parts:
Part One: *OM. bhur bhuva svah*

Part Two: *Tat savitur varenyam*

Bhargo Devasya Dhimahi

Part Three: *Dhiyo yonah prachodayat.*

The first part harmonizes the vehicles; the second part causes aspiration, upliftment, and focus; the third part opens the pathway toward the Sun and invites us to surrender and fuse ourselves with the innermost light.

The first part refers not only to the physical, astral, and mental worlds but also to the etheric body, the emotional body, and the mental vehicle of man. These three vehicles are harmonized and brought into alignment with the three worlds by the first part of the Gayatri.

>OM. Bhur Bhuva Svah

or

>OM. Earth, Mid-world, and Heaven.

Tradition tells us that the sound of these *Sanskrit* words has power to harmonize, align, and integrate the three vehicles of man with the three worlds. This power is called *mantra Shakti*, or energy emanation from words and sounds. Further, these three words refer to the three Deities ruling over these three spheres: Agni, Vaju, and Aditya and their energies: will, love, and light. In the *Upanishads* we read that the essence of the *Vedas* is also referred to by these three words, *Bhur, Bhuva, Svah*, which originate in the OM and have their existence in OM, which stands as the jewel in the Lotus or as the developing, unfolding human soul or Self.

The Analysis of the Gayatri

>OM

As we sound the OM we centralize ourselves within the most sacred core of our being and enter into deep silence, opening our hearts like a lotus to the Cosmic inspiration and bliss. Pantanjali says, "Let there be soundless repetition of OM and meditation there on." "Thence come the awakening of interior consciousness, and the removal of barriers."

>*Yoga Sutras of Patanjali*, I, (1: 28, 29)

>*All you who are on earth*

This is an invitation to all beings living on earth. Whether or not they hear the call, it penetrates their being and eventually evokes responses in those who are on the path of progress.

These words are uttered in deepest compassion and with a great sense of synthesis, subjectively calling all men to their highest duty. In addition to those who are living on the earth there are beings who live in the Mid-World. This term refers to the astral plane on which dwell those who have left their bodies or are in process of reincarnating and are closely related to the subjective world. These beings are sensitive to our feelings, imagination, and love. Since the astral plane is the plane of glamor, this invitation brings a great release to the inhabitants of the Mid-World. They need to be oriented into the light and liberated from their fantasies, glamor, and dreams of which the atmosphere of the astral plane is formed.

This call, when done properly, in concentration, and with a heartfelt sincerity, reaches the inhabitants of the astral plane and urges them to unite in meditation with the beings from whom the call emanates. This will be of tremendous assistance to those souls who, though caught on the astral plane, are striving to work out their own liberation.

The lights emanating from the being sending the call of meditation will guide the soul on the astral plane out of the dreams and glamors of that plane. This light, radiated at the time of deep meditation, serves as a torch to lead the dwellers on the astral plane out of darkness into the light of reality.

Heaven is the sphere of the mental plane inhabited by those who have graduated from the astral plane. But this plane may also be a trap because of the great joy, freedom, and bliss contained within its sphere. Many souls are content to remain there longer than is necessary and hesitate to return to earth to work out their past karmas through service, toil, and suffering, thereby furthering their own evolution.

The call also goes to beings on the mental plane inviting them to come and meditate. This may be likened to the ringing of a great bell inviting people to enter the sanctuary of meditation. These calls cannot fail to reach those who are in any way associated with us physically, emotionally, and mentally whether they be on objective or subjective planes.

The object of such a call is to

Let us meditate
Upon the light adorable
Of the divine Sun of life.

The divine Sun is the Central Spiritual Sun, the True Self of the Solar System from which are emitted those rays of wisdom and energy which lead us back to our Source, the Sun of Life.

According to esoteric wisdom there is the physical sun which is the light of the solar system. Then there is the Heart of the Sun from which radiate electromagnetic energies of attraction and love. There is also the Central Spiritual Sun which is as the Monad, the true spiritual Core of the system and from which emanates the principle of life.

The last sentence,

"Which may enlighten our Souls," is the conclusion of the Gayatri and the goal of meditation. In the original *Sanskrit* the word "*dhiyah*" refers to our discriminative faculty which, in a sense, is the human soul.

The enlightenment of the human soul is a gradual process. Meditation upon the inner Sun builds the channel through which light descends into the human soul whereby man is enabled to discriminate between the real and the unreal.

The first great enlightenment occurs when, through meditation, the intuitional light illumines the entire sphere of the mental plane and man takes the first higher initiation — the Transfiguration — in which he comes to realize that his identity is one with the Central Spiritual Sun. This light enters the mind gradually as a result of the service and meditation of the individual and leads him into illumination and realization. Man cannot live according to the principles he teaches, nor according to the laws he accepts unless the light of intuition penetrates his mental atmosphere. When this occurs, the age-long identification with man's lower bodies and their inertia, glamor, and illusions drop away and he sees himself "face to face."

In *Yajnavalkya Samita* is found a beautiful verse referring to the light which reads

> *The spiritual light which is hidden*
> *within the Sun is the light adorable.*
> *It shines through the hearts of all*
> *creatures as their consciousness.*
> *The spiritual light which shines through*
> *the physical sun shines through the hearts*
> *of every human soul.*
> *The light which shines in the heart*
> *of all human souls in the form of*
> *consciousness shines also through*
> *the universe, which as a*
> *heavenly man is a living organism.*

In the *Isavas Upanishad* 15 we find

> *O Lord, you nourish and*
> *sustain all that exists.*

*Please remove
the disk of the shining sun
so that as I travel on the path,
I see your face behind the
Veil of the Sun*

In esoteric books we are told that the physical sun provides fire by friction, the Heart of the Sun gives us the Solar Fire, and from the Central Spiritual Sun comes the spiritual-electrical fire.

The Gayatri not only focuses our attention and consciousness upon the Central Spiritual Sun, from which emanate the life currents, but also invites us to focus, through meditation, upon the Central Core, the True Self within each being. This is the true North by which all the directions of our life's ship are controlled. Those who meditate and gradually come closer to this Central Self will find that their physical problems will be dissolved, their glamors, daydreams, and illusions will be eliminated, and they will start on the pure Path of the Divine Sun. They will follow this path in the light of their Spiritual Selves and gradually become detached from their pseudo-selves, egos, urges, and drives and stand in the light of their true destination.

As a result of this enlightenment, the spiritual evolution of the meditators progresses and they take their next step on the path of reality. Those who dwell on the astral plane move forward, and those who are enchanted in the heavenly world proceed to the path of duty and responsibility on the physical or another plane.

This group meditation, entered into in conjunction with beings either in the physical body or out of the body, accomplishes a great upsurge towards the Sun, sheds light into the human soul, and challenges the meditator to advance toward his Cosmic destiny.

Some people believe that the repetition of the Gayatri by itself brings results. This is not so. It is the repetition of the mantram combined with meditation upon the Central Spiritual Sun that releases man from his age-long prison and admits him on the path of his divine heritage

The Gayatri is a seed thought of advanced disciples and Initiates who, after a long life of meditation and service, eventually reach the realization that the manifested universe is the expression of the Central Spiritual Sun which is the True Self of the universe. Gradually all their meditation focuses upon the supreme seed thought: the Central Spiritual Sun in the universe and in man. They may meditate upon any subject as long as it is a part of the expression of the Great Central Sun, the Self.

Through such meditation will man gradually contact his inner core and begin to live and express himself as that inner core, his Self.

— 5 —

The Prayer to Shamballa

Thou Who called me to the path of labor,
Accept my ableness and my desire.
Accept my labor, O Lord,
Because by day and by night
Thou beholdest me.
Manifest Thy hand, O Lord,

Because great is the darkness.
I follow Thee!

Agni Yoga Society, *Agni Yoga*, para. 104.

The disciple of the new era is striving to reach a level of spiritual purity on which he can contact the highest communication center between the planet and solar system.

Shamballa is a vortex of spiritual energies which passes to our planet not only life-giving energies of the Sun and of Cosmic sources, but also it is the center which sets for us the Purpose toward which strive all the kingdoms of Nature. It is the captain of the planetary ship.

In ancient books Shamballa is referred to as the Stronghold, the Tower, the Sacred Island, Kalapa, etc. The name Shamballa means the happy land or the land of bliss. This center, according to the Ancient Wisdom, is formed by very high degree Initiates Who act as intermediators between Hierarchy and Shamballa and between Shamballa and Solar Lives. The ruler of Shamballa is a great Being Who is called by many names: Sanat Kumara, the Ancient of Days, the Rigden Jyepo, etc. He came from a sacred planet to help the evolution of our planet under the guidance of the Planetary Logos. The prayer to Shamballa is directed to Him, the Lord and the King of the world.

Thou Who called me to the path of labor.

The Ageless Wisdom teaches that when a man is ready and purified enough throughout his personality and is in contact with the True Self, for the first time this great Being contacts and initiates him into the mysteries of the Transfiguration. This is the Third Initiation of esoteric books and is experienced at the time when the call goes to him for the great labor, labor for one humanity and for all the kingdoms of Nature. It is at this stage of the path that the Initiate sees the star of his life and sets himself on the path toward a great purpose.

Accept my ableness and my desire.

The Initiate puts all that he is and all that he has on the altar of sacrifice, including all his desires. To Initiates, desire is an ever-growing urge to achieve perfection and unity with the whole. All these are dedicated to the Lord.

Life after life this dedicated life-focus continues with greater service and sacrifice, with less illusions, glamors, and vanities, until one day the Initiate can stand again in the presence of the great One and say,

Accept my labor, O Lord.

I am standing in front of You with great labor, done in Your name, for the great purpose that You have in Your heart. The labor I did was as the Labor of Hercules, and now I am confident that I have done it well. The proof will be Your acceptance of my gift to You: my labor.

Because by day and by night Thou beholdest me.

Your presence was and is always with me. Since You called me to the Great Labor, not for a single moment were You absent from my mind. I saw Your eyes everywhere, I heard Your call everywhere in all my striving and Labor, and that is why I have a great Labor to bring again to Your altar of sacrifice.

Manifest Thy hand, O Lord, because great is darkness.

Though I see Your eyes and hear Your voice within me and in everything, everywhere, yet Thy power is needed in the world to dispel the darkness in which all beings live. It is the darkness of ignorance. It is the darkness of separatism, the darkness of greed and exploitation, the darkness of pain and suffering. *Manifest Thy hand, O Lord.* Your hand is the energy which as lightning flashes out from Shamballa and creates purification, synthesis, and brotherhood.

Once Your hand manifested Itself and the Lemurian continent ceased to exist. Another time Your hand manifested and Atlantis with all its civilization disappeared into the ocean. Another time when Your hand manifested we had the great World Wars, the release of atomic energy, and the formulation of the United Nations and human rights.

And Your hand manifested again at the Full Moon of Taurus in 1975. Let that manifestation bring unity, synthesis, brotherhood, and universality and wipe away all separation, all greed, all exploitation, all hypocrisy, and all hatred, and lead us into Brotherhood of humanity.

I follow Thee.

I am ready for any labor, any sacrifice, any service. I want to follow Thee. I want to fulfill Your Plan, Your Purpose. I follow Thee in all my ways, in all my responses. I follow Thee, my Lord, by doing good, creating beauty, being in truth. These are my steps toward You. The highest destiny toward which You are going is my destiny, being a cell in Your body. I follow Thee in focusing my life upon the vision that You released in me by Your actual beauty, and with one pointed striving, labor, and concentration I will try to unfold Your Self in me and Myself in You, aflame with Cosmic Vision.

Let my prayer be
> *"Thee, O Lord, I shall*
> *serve in everything,*
> *always and everywhere.*
> *Let my path be marked*
> by the attainment of selflessness."
>
> Agni Yoga Society, *Fiery World,* Vol. III, para. 7.

Part II
Prayers, Mantrams & Invocations

The Lord's Prayer

*Our Father Who art in heaven, Hallowed be Thy
  name.
Thy kingdom come.
Thy will be done on earth as it is in heaven.
Give us this day our daily bread.
And forgive us our debts, as we forgive our
  debtors.
And lead us not into temptation, but deliver us
  from evil. For Thine is the kingdom, and the
  power, and the glory, for ever. Amen.*

Matthew 6:9-13

Prayer on the way to the Sacred and Hallowed Dwelling

*O Lord of my spirit, forsake not the pilgrim!
The Guru hastens not to shelter me from
  the storm which threatens.
The pain will pierce the depths of my heart.
And the veil of the whirlwind
  will hide the light of Thy Face.*

With Thee I fear not my ignorance.
The phantoms reveal not their faces.
Lead me upon the path, O Thou Blessed One.
Touch my eyes that I may see Thy Gates!

Agni Yoga Society, *Leaves of Morya's Garden,* Vol. I, para. 12.

My First Message

Thou who gavest the Ashram,
Thou who gavest two lives,
Proclaim.
Builders and warriors, strengthen the steps.
Reader, if thou hast not grasped — read again,
   after a while.
The predestined is not accidental,
And the leaves fall off in due time.
Yet the winter is but the messenger of spring.
All is revealed; all is attainable.
I shall cover you with a shield — labor.
I have spoken.

Agni Yoga Society, *Leaves of Morya's Garden,* Vol. I

The Resplendent Temple

We lay stones for the steps
   to the resplendent Temple.
In the name of Christ we carry the rocks.
Erect Thy Altar, O Lord, in our garden.
The rocks are too large for the garden.
Too steep the steps for the flowers.

On a cloud He approaches.
On the grass shall He sit beside us.

I rejoice, O Lord, to give to Thee my garden.
Depart not, O Manifested Lord.
Desert not our garden.
With stars is Thy Path adorned.
Among them shall I find Thy Way.
I shall follow Thee — My Lord.
Should the worldly sun disperse Thy starry signs,
Then shall I invoke the aid of
  storm and wave to veil its rays.
Wherein its use if it obscure
  Thy starry tokens?

Agni Yoga Society, *Leaves of Morya's Garden*, Vol. I, para. 73.

The Messenger

Creator, let my spirit be revived
  when the storm abates,
Thunder fills the silence of the night,
  and lightning crosses my window.
Can it be that even during such
  a night the Messenger will come?
But I know my question is a forward one.
The Messenger is coming.
Master, my mind is dull with sleep
  and my eyes penetrate not the darkness.
I will place a hammer at my door.
Let the Messenger shatter the bolt.
Wherefore shall I need a lock after
  the coming of the Messenger?

Agni Yoga Society, *Leaves of Morya's Garden*, Vol. I, para. 295.

Teacher

*Thou who gavest the voice and shield to me,
send a Teacher upon my paths —
my heart is open.*

Agni Yoga Society, *Leaves of Morya's Garden,* Vol. I, para. 243.

Preparedness

*Wherefore, O Lord, dost Thou not trust me
to gather the fruits of Thy Garden?
— But where are thy baskets?*

*Why, O Lord, dost Thou not pour upon me
the streams of Thy Bliss?
— But where are thy pitchers?*

*O Lord, why dost Thou whisper
and not proclaim Thy Truth in thunder?
— But where are thy ears?
It were better, moreover, to hearken
to the thunder amidst the mountains.*

Agni Yoga Society, *Leaves of Morya's Garden,* Vol. I, para. 296.

Strength to my Heart

*O Lord, give strength to my heart
and power to my arm.*

Because I am Thy servant.
In Thy Rays I shall learn the eternal Truth of Being.
In Thy Voice I shall listen to the harmony of the World.
My heart I give to Thee, O Lord.
Sacrifice it for the sake of the world.

Agni Yoga Society, *Leaves of Morya's Garden,* Vol. I, para. 317.

My Presence

O Lord of my prayers,
  be merciful to me in my striving.
Rebuke me not for my transgressions.
My spirit sings the song — Thy Song.
But my body is weary and my limbs obey me not.

Pupil, thy body must not hinder thee upon the path.

Master, I see Thy Face, I behold Thy Mercy.

Pupil, I am here, but in thy blindness
  thou didst forget My Presence.

Agni Yoga Society, *Leaves of Morya's Garden,* Vol. I, para. 320.

The Creator

O Thou Creator of the Universe,
Thou Summit of Heaven, Glory of Glories!

Great Unmanifested in the Beginning,
Manifested at the End!
Yea, yea, yea!
Where is the Beginning, where the End?

Agni Yoga Society, *Leaves of Morya's Garden*, Vol. I, para. 329.

Thy Benevolence

O Lord, Thou gavest me Thy Benevolence
*　to safeguard.*
Thou has taught me how to guard It.
And now teach me how to return that which I
*　have guarded at Thy Call, O Lord.*

Agni Yoga Society, *Leaves of Morya's Garden*, Vol. I, para. 381.

Lotus Flower

Thou Blossom of the Lotus Flower,
Dream of Dreams,
Seven-Pointed Pearl!
In Thee is hidden the knowledge of the universe.
In Thee is born the striving to behold the
*　mysteries.*

Hidden Temple of the Unknown,
Giver of Living Waters,
Great Healer of the Universe,
Soul ever-watchful over worldly terrors!
In Thy Light bathes Thy faithful servant,
Who has chosen Thee to be his whole possession.

O Lord of the Wisdom of Heavenly Gates,
Erect Thy Throne upon the topmost mountain.
Thence wilt Thou better see
  the fear and anguish of human hearts.

O Lord named the Compassionate,
Behold Thy sons engulfed in human darkness.
Darkness, darkness, darkness.
Light, light, light.
Without the darkness there would be no light,
For only in darkness may we behold the light.
But where abideth He, the Lord,
There is nor light, nor darkness.
All is One.
Mystery of Mysteries.
Holy of Holies.
Unapproached by men, It remains pure;
But realized by human minds,
Its luster dulls.
Such is the law.
Follow the banner of battle.

Agni Yoga Society, *Leaves of Morya's Garden,* Vol. I, para. 327.

Seven Words

In the morning, repeating the seven words, say:
"Help us lest we pass Thy Labor."
And repeating My Name,
  and asserting thyself in My Labor,
Thou wilt attain My Day.

Agni Yoga Society, *Leaves of Morya's Garden,* Vol. I, para. 388.

My Mantram

So long a time did I prepare.
So long did I wait for my mantram.
Still, it is short.
Turn not from me, O Lord!
Naught can I add to this word.

And now my conjuration:
O Lord, Thou shalt not forsake me.
I will find Thee.
I know all Thy abodes.
Thou art in all!

Be merciful, My Lord.
My prayer is simple.
Short is my mantram and forward is my
  conjuration.
But if I cannot leave Thee,
Thou canst not hide Thee from my sight.
My ear is aware of Thy Step.
My mouth is sweet with Thy Divine Savor.
Thou art my nurture.
Shall I have time to conjure Thee,
  O Lord?

I fear lest my prayer displease Thee,
And my mantram be not acceptable.
But I will retain in my hands Thy Garment.
O My Lord, I will be daring,
And by audacity will win the ocean of happiness.
Because I wish it.

Agni Yoga Society, *Leaves of Morya's Garden*, Vol. I, para. 342.

To the Light

It is time to say to the Light:
  "I come as thy helper, and
  to the sun itself
  I will stretch out my hand.
  And as long as the silver thread is
  intact, the stars themselves
  shall be my armor."

Agni Yoga Society, *Leaves of Morya's Garden*, Vol. II, p. 162.

Wither my Hand

Father, wither my hand
  if it be raised for an unworthy deed!
Father, turn to ashes my brain if it recoil in
  treacherous thought!
Father, demolish my being
  if it be turned to evil!

My son, I shall not touch thy hand.
My son, I shall not harm thy brain
  if thou art on the way to an achievement.
But amidst attainment devote a time
  to silence of the spirit.
Then shall I approach thy inner being.
The seed of the Great Silence
  leads to the knowledge of the Great Service.

Father, henceforth I will shorten my psalms,

And I will limit the length of my hymns.
And achievement shall be my prayer,
And I will start it with silence.

Agni Yoga Society, *Leaves of Morya's Garden,* Vol. I, para. 360.

Thy Country

I will help to build Thy Country,
in the Name of the Mother of the World
and of My Father!

Agni Yoga Society, *Leaves of Morya's Garden,* Vol. II, pp.169-170

Invoke Me

My Spirit knows how the power is being forged.
I advise not to pray to Me but
to invoke Me.
And My Hand will not delay in
manifesting Itself in the battle.

Agni Yoga Society, *Leaves of Morya's Garden,* Vol. II, pages 171-172.

Pure Thought

A pure thought ever ascends.
At the feet of Christ it blossoms, radiant.
With pure blue flame glows the Calling Word
and radiates the Chalice of Exaltation.
O Lord, drain our tears and

perceive the flame of our heart.
"By flames shall I dry thy tears and upraise
the Temple of the heart."
Leaves of Morya's Garden, Vol. I, para. 21.

Wings of Alaya

Lord, grant me to cast into the flames
  the deceptive rags of the customary.
I shall not err in realizing that
  winged daring has Thy blessing.
In the sacred furnace shall I forge the wings of
  Alaya.
Unknown to me are complaints, cruelty,
  or aught that could weigh down my new wings.
New shall be my song!
Agni Yoga Society, Agni Yoga, para. 11.

Seven Gates

Lord of the Seven Gates,
  lead us sunwards who have passed through the
    midnight.
Thine are our arrows, O Lord.
Without Thy Command we shall not
  enter the city of rest.
Neither an hour, nor a day, nor a
  year will arrest our way;
Because Thou, the most speedy,
  holdest the reins of our horses.

*Because Thou also passed this way
 and gave Thy patience as guarantee.
Tell us, Keeper, whence flows the
 stream of patience?*

"Out of the mine of trust."

Agni Yoga Society, Agni Yoga, para. 117.

Veiled Her Face

*Teacher, I have succeeded in
 withstanding the stabs of heat
 and the horror of cold.
My bodily strength has left me,
 but my ear is open.
And the body of light is ready to tremble at Your
 call.
And my arms are ready to carry the
 heaviest stones for the Temple.
Three Names are known to me.
Known to me is the Name of
 Her Who Veiled Her Face.
My strength is magnified.*

Agni Yoga Society, Agni Yoga, para. 125.

Accept my Arms

*Lord, accept my arms,
 the smiting sword and the shield of defense.
How weighty is my helmet,*

which in the battle was lighter than a feather!
My sandals burden my steps and
my armlets are as chains on my wrists.

Agni Yoga Society, *Agni Yoga*, para. 223.

The Crossroads

How then, O Lord, to spread Thy Teaching?
How then, O Lord, to find those
to whom it is predestined to
apply Thy Word for fulfillment?

And the Lord said in reminder,
"A hermit searched for him to whom to entrust
the Revelation.
And he took the scroll and placed it on the
crossroad, 'Let the Higher One Himself point out
who should find His Ordainments.'

"And a little girl came and wrapped her bread
in the scroll of Scriptures.
But the hermit prepared another scroll
And again placed it on the crossroad.

"And a merchant passed,
and covered the scroll with the figures of his
revenue.
But the hermit did not tire, and
once more placed a scroll.
And thus until the very end
of his works and his day.

"But when the Higher One asked him
how he had spread the Teaching,
he answered,
'It is not given unto me to judge
which bird will build the best nest
of these ordainments.'

"Thus, we never know who will give the scroll
for torment, who for oblivion,
and who will place it under his pillow
in order to affirm upon it his own foundation.

"I do not consider that thou has acted wrongly
in giving thy labor for use
to those unknown to thee."

Thus the Lord affirmed
the spreading of the Teaching impersonally,
without impatience, without irritation, without
  expectation.

Thus, give ye also, Without prejudice to whom ye
  give,
without pronouncing the everyday judgment.

Carry, O bird, the Teaching;
and in thy flight drop it into the hearth
of those who live in expectation of receiving it.

Carry the Teaching to the crossroad!
Agni Yoga Society, Agni Yoga, para. 669.

Let Thy Prayer Be

Let thy prayer be — "Thee, O Lord,
  I shall serve in everything,
  always and everywhere.
Let my path be marked by the
  attainment of selflessness...."

There is inscribed upon the Shield of Light —
"Lord,
  I come alone,
  I come in manifested achievement,
  I shall reach the goal,
  I shall reach it!"

Agni Yoga Society, Fiery World, Vol. III, para. 7.

Mother of the World

The Mother of the World is the
  great creative force in our being.
Thou hast abided in the cults of
  the ancients as earth, as sun,
  as fire, as air, as water.
Thou, the All-bestowing!
Thou, the All-revealing!
Thou who hast made manifest to humanity
  the great and joyous realization
  of the Mother!
Thou who hast indicated achievement
  and who hast veiled thy Image!
Thou who hast manifested to us
  the Fire of Space!
Thou who hast taken upon thy shoulders

the burden of human actions!
We beseech Thee, restore to us
  our lost smile!
Grant us mastery of the sacred
  Fiery Might!

Agni Yoga Society, *Infinity,* Vol. I, para. 38.

I Love Thee, O Lord

... What can more strongly unify
  than the mantram —
"I love Thee, O Lord!"

Agni Yoga Society, *Fiery World,* Vol. II, para. 296.

The Great Hymn

I come again
  to greet and thank the League;

I come again
  to greet and thank the kindred;

I come again
  to greet and thank the warriors;

I come again
  to greet and thank the women,
  my forefathers...
  and what they established.

— 76 —

My forefathers — hearken to them!

From *Hiawatha and the Great Peace*, p. 208.

The Self

More radiant than the sun,
purer than the snow,
subtler than the ether —
is the Self,
the spirit within my heart;
I am that Self,
that SELF am I.

Aham eva parabrahma
Verily I am the Boundless.

Om tat sat
Om, that boundless Reality.

Beauty

In Beauty we are united,
through Beauty we pray,
with Beauty we conquer.

Nicholas Roerich

Go in Beauty

Go in Beauty
Beauty before you
Beauty behind you
Beauty to your right
Beauty to your left
Beauty above you
Beauty beneath you
Go in Beauty
In Beauty all is accomplished

       Navaho Invocation

Beauty in Your Life

Let beauty shine
in your eyes.
Let beauty flow
from your mouth.
Let beauty manifest
through your hands.
Let your spirit
always be inspired
by the beauty of stars.
Live in beauty.
Work in beauty.
Depart in beauty.

  From *Hiawatha and the Great Peace*, p. 205.

Mother

Mother of the World,
All-bestowing,
All-embracing,
we wish to adorn our far-off firmament!

Agni Yoga Society, Infinity, Vol. I, para. 18.

Help

No dogma can forbid conversing with
the Highest.
The more beautifully it is done,
the nearer will be the approach.
But if help is needed, it suffices to
express oneself with — "Help."
But even for such a simple word
attractiveness is needed.

Agni Yoga Society, Fiery World, Vol. II, para. 38.

Beauty of Infinity

Verily, I affirm the beauty
of Infinity!
I wish, O Lord, to sense the pulsation
of the grandeur of the Cosmos!

Agni Yoga Society, Infinity, Vol. II, para. 12.

Your Beauty

My Lord,
  let your beauty
  shine everywhere
  and bloom in every man.

My Lord,
  let your peace
  be spread in our hearts.

My Lord,
  let your love
  unite all mankind.

My Lord,
My Lord,
  the Light of the World.

Torkom Saraydarian

Divine Love

May divine love, light, and beauty
  be our daily breath and thought,
  and let light, love, and power
  restore the Plan on earth.

Lord of Beauty

O Lord of Beauty,
Let me stand in Your Temple

of color supernal,
And within the Symphonies divine.
May I achieve harmony with the
  Heart of the Cosmic rhythm,
And radiate the uplifting,
  expanding Beauty of that Heart
  in all my actions, aspirations, and visions.

Living Sacrifice

The living Sacrifice of the world.
The living Beauty on our path.
The Resurrection and fiery fountain
  of love and life.
I come to Thee with a pure heart
  and surrender myself
  to You —
  for the service of humanity
  for the fulfillment of the Plan,
  for the glory of Your reappearance.

I stand in Your Presence.
Charge me with the Spirit of love,
  of light, and power,
That I may follow Your Path
  of resurrection,
  of sacrifice,
  of love.

More Radiant

More radiant than the sun,
Purer than the snow,
Subtler than the ether,
Is the Self,
The spirit within my heart.
I am that Self,
That Self am I.

May the energy of the Divine Self infuse me,
   and the light of the Soul direct.
May I walk in that light.
May that light shine upon my way.
May I pour forth that light
   on others.

May the energy of my Divine Self
   inspire me,
And the light of my Soul direct.
May I be led,
  from darkness to Light,
  from the unreal to the Real,
  from death to Immortality,
  from chaos to Beauty.

River of Miracles

O Thou, the river of miracles
   within me,
Pour the healing waters of
   compassion

*on the wounded body of humanity
and make man whole.*

OM   OM   OM

O Great Spirit

*O Great Spirit,
Whose voice I hear in the winds,
  and whose breath gives life to all the world,
Hear Me!
I am small and weak, I need your
  strength and wisdom.*

*Let me walk in beauty, and make my
  eyes ever behold the red and
  purple sunset.*

*Make my hands respect the things
  you have made and my ears
  sharp to hear your voice.*

*Make me wise so that I may understand
  the things you have taught my people.*

*Let me learn the lessons you have
  hidden in every leaf and rock.*

*I seek strength, not to be greater than
  my brother, but to fight my greatest enemy —
  myself.
Make me always ready to come to you
with clean hands and straight eyes,*

so when life fades,
  as the fading sunset,
my spirit may come to you without shame.

An Indian Prayer

Dedication

(If recited in a group, hold hands.)

We the members of this Group,
We are one in essence.
  May our souls rejoice.
We are one with Humanity.
  May our souls rejoice.
We are one with all Life Forms.
  May our souls rejoice.
We are one with the Sun.
  May our souls rejoice.
We are one with the Life of the Galaxy.
  May our souls rejoice.
We are one with the Stars.
  May our souls rejoice.
We are one with Infinity.
  *May our **Spirits** rejoice.*

Torkom Saraydarian

Group Brothers

I am one with my group brothers,
  and all that I have is theirs.

May the love which is in my soul
  pour forth to them.
May the strength which is in me
  lift and aid them.
May the thoughts which my soul creates
  reach and encourage them.

As the One Sun

As the one Sun illumines all this world,
  so do I.
The Self,
The Knower of the Field,
  lights up the whole field.
Light of Lights also am I called.
Beyond the darkness am I.
I am Wisdom.
I am the aim of Wisdom.
I am gained by Wisdom.
In the heart am I set firm.

Bhagavad Gita 13: 33-34

Mantram of the New Group of World Servers

May the Power of the One Life
  pour through the group of
  all true servers.
May the Love of the One Soul
  characterize the lives of all who seek to aid the
  Great Ones.

*May I fulfill my part
in the One Work
through self-forgetfulness,
harmlessness, and right speech.*

        Alice A. Bailey, *A Treatise on White Magic*, p. 261

Prayer of Saint Francis of Assisi

*Lord —Make me an instrument of Your peace.
Where there is hatred, let me sow love;
Where there is injury, pardon;
Where there is doubt, faith;
Where there is despair, hope;
Where there is darkness, light;
And where there is sadness, joy.
O, Divine Master,
Grant that I may not so much seek
  to be consoled as to console;
  to be understood as to understand;
  to be loved as to love;
For it is in giving that we receive;
It is in pardoning that we are pardoned;
And it is in dying that we are born
  to Eternal Life.*

The Sun

*O Lord,
  You nourish and sustain
  all that exists.*

Please remove the disk of the shining sun,
  so that as I travel on the path,
  I see Your face,
  behind the
  veil of the Sun.

                              Isavas Upanishad 15

Invocation to the Solar Angel

May the words of my mouth
And the meditation of my heart
Be always acceptable in Thy sight,
O my Soul, my Lord, and my Redeemer.

Money for the Forces of Light

O Thou in Whom we live and move
  and have our being,
The Power that can make all things new,
Turn to spiritual purposes
  the money in the world;
Touch the hearts of men everywhere
  so that they may give
  to the work of the Hierarchy
  that which has hitherto
  been given to material satisfaction.
The New Group of World Servers needs money in
  large quantities.
I ask that the needed vast sums
  may be made available.

*May this potent energy of Thine
be in the hands of the Forces of Light.*

Alice A. Bailey, *Discipleship in the New Age*, Vol. II, p. 229.

Love of the Lord

*I am surrounded by the Love of
the Lord Christ [or any Great One]
as by a sphere of fire,
that burns up all evil that approaches
and goes out in the love to all.*

(*As you are sounding this mantram, visualize the protecting fire.*)

Mantram of Peace

*May the Holy Ones,
Whose pupils we aspire to become,
Show us the Light we seek;
Give us the strong aid of
  Their compassion
  and Their wisdom.
There is a peace that passeth
  understanding;
It abides in the hearts of those
  who live in the eternal.
There is a power that makes all things new;
It lives and moves in those who
  know the Self as One.
May that peace brood over us,
That power uplift us,*

Till we stand where the One Initiator is invoked,
Till we see His Star shine forth.

Invocation for the United Nations

May the Peace and the Blessings of the Holy Ones
pour forth over the worlds
  —rest upon the United Nations,
  on the work and the workers,
protecting,
purifying,
energizing,
and strengthening.
There is a Peace which passeth understanding.
It abides in the hearts of those who live in the
  Eternal.
There is a Power that maketh all things new.
It lives and moves in those who know the Self as
  One.
May the Rhythm of the Peace vibrate within the
  United Nations
  and in the heart of every worker.
May the Rhythm of that Creative Power
  resound within the United Nations,
  and in the lives of all who serve there —
  awakening,
  transmuting,
  and giving birth to that which ought to be.
May the Chalice the United Nations is building
  become a focal point for the descent of spiritual
  force,
  which filling it and overflowing

to the world draws towards itself
all those whose work lies there.
May the consciousness of the United Nations
become ever more at-one,
the many lights One Light,
in the Light of the Self.
May the aspiration and the dedication
of the United Nations burn as a
clear flame in the service of Humanity.
May the Love and the Light and the Life
of the One Life pour through the United
Nations,
cleansing it from all evil,
and attracting all good.

The Blessing of the Beloved Kwan Yin — Goddess of Mercy

May the Peace of God be upon this household!
May the Love of God be in your hearts.
May the Light of God be in your souls!
May the Wisdom of God be in your minds!
May the Virtue and Purity of God be in your
  feelings!
May the Strength and Vitality of God
  be among the members of your household!
May the Health and Well-Being of God
  be manifest through the bodies,
  the garments which you wear!
May the Grace of God be in your worship!
May the Talents and Genius of God be manifest
  through your senses!

*May the fullness of the Victory of
your own God Plan be manifest
through your souls at the close of your earth
life!*

Joy, Bliss, and Peace

*Let joy, bliss, and peace
be spread upon the world.*

Dedication of the Soul

*In the center of the will of God
I stand.
Naught shall deflect my will from His.
I implement that will by love.
I turn towards the field of service.
I, the Triangle divine, work out
that will within the square
and serve my fellow man.*

Almighty Power

*O Almighty Power,
may Your peace
pour into me
and build a shield
and may Your Power
radiate through me.*

Prayer of Protection

My Lord,
  shield us with Your Light,
  shield our home with your Light,
  protect us when we walk, fly, drive.
May Your Hand be upon me, my family members,
  group members,
  Teacher,
  and the world.

Prayer for Purification

My Lord,
  let Your Fire purify my mind and cleanse all ugly
  and dark thoughts existing in my mind.

My Lord,
  let Your Fire purify my heart,
  and burn all feelings that are
  negative, painful, and separative.

My Lord,
  restore Your Fire in my heart.
  Give me courage,
  and let Your Fire shine in all my
  thoughts, feelings, and actions.
Fill all my being with Love and Bliss,
  so that I radiate Your Presence.

                                        Torkom Saraydarian

Prayer of Inspiration

(Holding hands together in prayer form, touch your hands to your head and then your heart for each of the first three verses.)

*My Lord,
inspire and charge me with Your Spirit.
Let me walk the path of beauty, goodness, and
 righteousness.*

*My Lord,
inspire and charge me
so that I commit myself
for the service of my nation and humanity.*

*My Lord,
inspire and charge me
so that I live as a disciple,
and fulfill Your Will in everything and
 everywhere.
 [Visualize a chalice above your head full of light
 — blue, gold, yellow.]*

*My Lord,
let this Chalice be filled with Your Fire,
so that I live with the fire
of enthusiasm, in the field of Your service.
AUM AUM AUM*

Torkom Saraydarian, June 10, 1986, Discipleship Seminar.

Salutations

Salutations to my Inner Guide;
  gratitude for Your long and lasting guidance
  for many lives.
May I be led in Your blessing
  from darkness to Light.

Love Each Other

Love each other,
Love each other,
Love each other,
Love to all.

There's a Jewel in your heart,
Radiating Beauty.
Our hearts fly toward Beauty.

We stand for humanity,
We stand for all creation,
We stand for the coming Christ,
Who will reveal peace, joy, light,
  simplicity, unity.

Torkom Saraydarian

Living Flame

O Living Flame,
  Glory to Thee,
  Glory to Thee.

O Living Flame
  in every heart,
  Glory to Thee,
  Glory to Thee!

O Living Flame,
  Glory to Thee.
  Glory to Thee.
  Glory to Thee.

In Every Heart
  Glory to Thee,
  Glory to Thee,
  Glory to Thee,
  Glory to Thee,
  Glory to Thee,
  Glory to Thee,
  Glory to Thee.

Torkom Saraydarian

Love to all Beings

Love to all beings,
  North, South,
  East, West,
  above, below.
Love to all beings.

Compassion to all beings,
   North, South,
   East, West,
   above, below.
Compassion to all beings.

Joy to all beings,
   North, South,
   East, West,
   above, below.
Joy to all beings.

Serenity to all beings,
   North, South,
   East, West,
   above, below.
Serenity to all beings.

Your Presence

O Lord,
   make us to feel Your Presence
   within us,

And in Your Presence let us know
   what really we are.

Your Presence, within Us.

Asatoma

Asatoma, satga maya
Tama soma joy tirga maya
Mri torma, mri tanga maya

Lead us, O Lord, from darkness to Light,
   From the unreal to the Real,
   From death to Immortality,
   From chaos to Beauty.

Beloved Lord

Beloved Lord,
Almighty God,
Through the rays of the sun,
Through the waves of the air,
Through the all-pervading Fire in space,
Purify me,
Revivify me,
And I pray,
Heal my body, heart, and mind.

OM

A Sufi Prayer

Searching for You

I am on the way to search for You.
You are here, close to me.
You are there — far, far away from me.

Deeper I go within me,
Closer You are to me.
Farther I am from me,
Farther You are from me.

Lord, Lord, You are in me.
Why so long, so long,
I longed for You?

Lord, Lord, You are in me.
Why so long, so long,
I longed for You?

Torkom Saraydarian

The Stars

The stars make me to grow,
  to raise my eyes toward the values of Future,
  toward the values of Infinity.

The stars give me joy,
  the spirit of striving.

Gratitude to the Source of Light!

The stars are paths,
  the stars are doors
  toward the most sacred Temple of Cosmos,
  Of Cosmos.

Filled with Joy

Let our hearts be filled with joy!
Let our hearts be filled with joy!

Joy opens our hearts.
  Joy brings us Light.
Joy is the door of the Lord.

Throw your ego into the ocean.
Let it melt away.
You exist only
  when your ego is gone
  into the ocean.

Only one who radiates all
  in his heart,
  only he exists.

Torkom Saraydarian

Group Worship

I love You, Lord,
I love You, Lord.

I love You, Lord, in my friends.
I love You, Lord, in my friends.

I love You, Lord, in all the Saints.
I love You, Lord, in all the Saints.

I love You, Lord, in all humanity.
I love You, Lord, in all humanity.

I love You, Lord, in all the stars.
I love You, Lord, in all the stars.

I love You, Lord, in all that exists.
I love You, Lord, in all that exists.

O, Self-revealing One, reveal Thyself in me.
O, Self-revealing One, reveal Thyself in me.

Torkom Saraydarian

Path to Infinity

O Lord,

You build a Path to Infinity.
You build a Path between man and man,
  between nation and nation.
You build a Path between You and Man.

You build a path between the sun and the atom —
  between man and the Cosmos.

You build the Path.

Joy Song

In joy I walk.
In joy I walk.

In joy I cool down.

In joy my eyes regain a power.
In joy my eyes regain a power.

In joy my head becomes serene.

In joy my legs regain a power.

In joy I hear, again, again.
In joy I hear, again, again.

In joy my blue spells are gone.

In joy I walk.
In joy I walk.
In joy I walk.
In joy I walk.

In beauty I walk.
In beauty I walk.
In beauty I walk.
I walk.
I walk.
I walk.

Torkom Saraydarian

Responsibility

May the sense of responsibility be developed in me
That I may rightly serve the Plan.

May the purity of vision, which sometimes I have felt,
Enable me to tread the Path of service.

May I stand free
And may I set free those I meet and love
That they, too, may rightly serve.

May the Divine Self inspire me
And the light of the Soul direct.
May I walk in that Light.
May that Light shine upon my way.
May I pour forth that Light on others.

The Light

I am one with the Light which shines
  through my Soul,
  my group brothers,
  and my Master.

This Light which is rooted in the healing love of the One Soul
radiates upon me and permeates every part of my body,
healing, soothing, strengthening, and dissipating all that hinders good health and service.

The Word

I am the Soul, the Word incarnate.
Through Life and Word and Deed I speak to
    men.
That radiance pure am I.
With the Light within
I tread the Lighted Way.
I hold aloft the Light
That others, too, may walk and see.

The Server

I am a server in the world of man,
Of that Brotherhood of Light,
Whose Life and Light sustain all in life
In this manifested Universe.
May my light so shine in harmony with Their
    Light,
Ere long the "Day be with us"
When those that wait shall be liberated
Into Light and Life of Peace.
To this I relinquish
All sense of limitation,
Taking my place in the ranks of Light bearers,
Who live only to bless and serve.

Unity

May the unity of all things be revealed to me.
May I be aware of the Oneness of Life.
May the beauty of oneness shine in my heart.

Fusion

*I stand within the harmonizing strain and stress,
And bring into fusion
The East and West, the North and South,
The form and the mind;
And radiate Beauty to build the Path
Of the Coming One.*

Lighted Way

*May the Light that is my Soul
   Dispel all glamour.*

*May the power of Love that is my Soul
   Release me from attachment.*

*May I be given strength to serve,
   That those I love
May tread the lighted way.*

Solar Angel

*O Thou Who watched me since my cradle
and shed Your Light upon me,
accept my gratitude
and love for You....*

My gratitude to You.
I will persist to come
closer and closer to You
until the day in which Your Glory
will shine in my eyes
and in my life.

Torkom Saraydarian. See *New Dimensions in Healing*, pp. 285-293, for complete prayer and method of contact.

Invoking Angels

O shining brothers of Light,
O magnetic servers of Love,
O carriers of the mighty Will of the Most High,
  here I present my heart to you
  with the fire of my aspiration,
  with the fire of my sincerity.
I call upon your help.

May your light enlighten me.
May your love heal me.
May the energy of the will you carry
  create integrity, harmony, and wholeness
  in all my being.

May I share your peace.
May I share your joy.
May I share your beauty.
May I share your freedom.

O shining brothers of Light,
  if it is the Will of the Most High,
  in the name of Christ
  let my body be healed.

Let my mind find the solution to problems.
Let my soul register the impressions of knowledge
  you want to pass to me.
Let your energy flow into me,
O shining brothers of Light.

I will use your light,
  your love,
  your energy imparted to me
  for the benefit of all humanity,
  for the manifestation
  of the Plan of Light and Love,
  for the fulfillment of the Divine Will.

I offer my gratitude to you
  as a fragrance
  rising from the altar of my heart.

May your blessed service expand
  all over the world.

May a chance be given to me
  to cooperate with your labor.
Gratitude and love to you.

Torkom Saraydarian, *New Dimensions in Healing,* pp. 560-562.

Thank You Lord

Thank You, Lord,
Thank You, Lord!

Thank You for the Sun.
Thank You for the oceans.

Thank You for the rivers.
Thank You, Lord.

Thank You, Lord,
for the blue sky and green mountains
and palpitating stars.
And thank You, Lord, for Your lakes.
Thank You, Lord.

Thank You, Lord,
for the rain and for the lightning.
And thank You, Lord,
for Your rainbows
and blooming flowers and trees.
Thank You, Lord.

Thank You, Lord,
for my friends.
Thank You, Lord, for their golden hearts.
Thank You, Lord.

Thank You, Lord,
for Your eyes.
Thank You, Lord.

Torkom Saraydarian

Affirmation

My Lord,
give me strength
and inspiration
to be beautiful,
to work for the beauty of others;

*to be good
and spread goodness
all the day;*

*to live in righteousness
and spread righteousness;*

*to spread joy
to everyone
and be joyful all the day;*

*to encourage freedom
in others
and be free in myself;*

*to be harmless
and not cause suffering
and pain to others;*

*to be aware
all the day
that Your eyes
watch me
and see all that
I do for others.*

*Lord, help me
to stand in Your Presence.*

Torkom Saraydarian, *Education as Transformation*, Vol. I, pp. 192-193.

A Daily Discipline of Worship — in five parts

Early Morning Worship

> *O Giver of Light,*
> *the Cosmic Beauty,*
> *permeate my whole nature*
> *with Thy Rays.*
>
> *Kindle the flame*
> *on the altar of my temple*
> *so that I may live*
> *as a beam of Light,*
> *in beauty,*
> *until the sunset of the day ...*
> *of my life.*

9 a.m. Worship

> *O sphere of Light,*
> *advancing and elevating Goodness,*
> *May my soul rise with You,*
> *expressing goodness in all its contacts.*

Noon Worship

> *The Flame of the Great Presence in me,*
> *let me stand as a radiant Fire of righteousness,*
> *today and during the days of my life.*
> *Let me think, act, and speak*
> *in the spirit of righteousness.*

Sunset Worship

> *My Lord,*
> *thank You for the joy of living today*
> *in the spirit of beauty, goodness, and*
> *righteousness.*

May Your joy radiate in other parts of the world,
  as the Sun disperses the night
  and brings the joy of the day.
My Lord,
  You are the joy of my heart.

Worship before Sleep

My Lord,
  let Your freedom permeate my whole being.
Let me be free from all worries and anxieties,
  from all painful memories of the day,
  from all attachments and identifications,
  so that my soul freely soars
  in Your Temple of Beauty.
Let me realize freedom from my
  physical, emotional, and mental crystallizations
  and be with You as a free soul.

Torkom Saraydarian

Lead Us O Lord

Lead us O Lord,
From darkness to Light,
From the unreal to the Real,
From death to Immortality,
From chaos to Beauty.
From the individual to the Universal
Fro m the many cycles to the One Life.
From manifestation to Space.
  Torkom Saraydarian, *Cosmos in Man,* p. 267.

Aham Eva Parabrahma

Verily I am the Boundless.

Om Tat Sat

Om, that boundless Reality.

Avira Virma Yedhi

O Self-Revealing One, reveal Thyself in me.

Om Mani Padme Hum

Salutations to the Jewel in the Lotus.

Grant me, O Lord, the mastery of self!
Agni Yoga Society, *Leaves of Morya's Garden*, Vol. I, para. 35.

Lord, accept my possessions if they be of use to Thee!
Agni Yoga Society, *Agni Yoga*, para. 261.

About the Publisher

T.S.G. Publishing Foundation, Inc. is a non-profit, tax exempt organization. Founded on November 30, 1987 in Los Angles, California, it relocated to Cave Creek, Arizona on January 1, 1994.

Our purpose is to be a pathway for self-transformation. We are fully devoted to publishing, teaching, and distributing the creative works of Torkom Saraydarian.

Our bookstore in Cave Creek and our online bookstore at our web site www.tsgfoundation.org offers the complete collection of the creative works of Torkom Saraydarian for sale and distribution.

Our newsletter *Outreach* contains thought-provoking articles and is available both in print and from our website with free email notification.

We also conduct weekly classes, special training seminars, and home study meditation courses offered on site and online at The Torkom Saraydarian University: www.TorkomSaraydarianUniversity.org

Ordering Information

The complete works of Torkom Saraydarian are available at TSG online or by telephone/fax.

Complete catalog of books, music, audio and video lectures available free online.

Contact us for any additional information:
— Printed Catalog
— Complete list of lecture tapes and videos
— Placement on mailing list for continuous updates
— A free copy of our newsletter *Outreach* by mail or email (latest edition and archived copies available on the website)
— *Free Wisdom* mailing list by email.
— **Join our Book Club. Contact us for details.**

T.S.G. Publishing Foundation, Inc.
P.O. Box 7068
Cave Creek, AZ 85327–7068
United States of America
TEL: (480) 502–1909
FAX: (480) 502–0713
E-Mail: info@tsgfoundation.org
Website: *www.tsgfoundation.org*

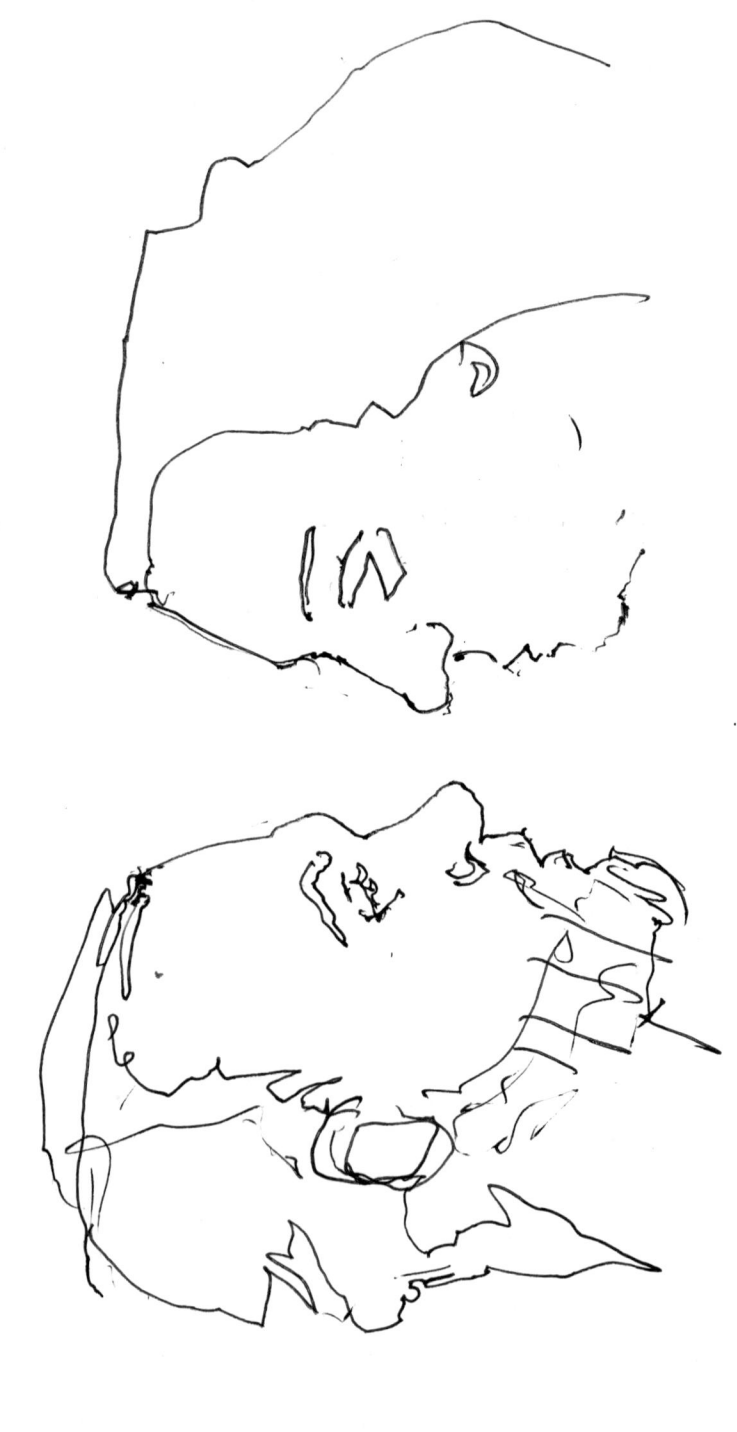